"Doug Fields knows his audience; he knows kids! *Too Old, Too Soon* WILL SERVE AS A USEFUL TOOL FOR YOUTH LEADERS, TEACHERS, AND PARENTS as they seek to mold and motivate a valuable generation."

—Tim Timmons
President, Game Plan for Living

"Doug Fields gives ample evidence in this book that he KNOWS WHAT'S GOING ON WITH YOUNG PEOPLE and how we should react to the mess they are in."

—Tony Campolo
Professor of Sociology, Eastern College and
Author, *It's Friday, but Sunday's Comin'*

"*Too Old, Too Soon* is an EXCELLENT RESOURCE. Doug Fields has a firm grasp on important issues parents should be dealing with and COMMUNICATES GREAT ADVICE in an effective way."

—Andy Stanley
Youth Pastor,
First Baptist Church
Atlanta, Georgia

"Doug Fields draws from his experience with students to give us VALUABLE INSIGHT into how the pressures of our culture are impacting our families."

—David Stoop, Ph.D.
Clinical Psychologist
Minirth-Meier-Stoop Clinic

"IF YOU ARE A PARENT of a teenager or younger child, YOU'LL LOVE THIS BOOK. It not only gives PRACTICAL INFORMATION on the way kids are, but takes A THOUGHTFUL LOOK AT WHY KIDS ARE THE WAY THEY ARE and what cultural influences are now shaping our children."

—Tic Long
President, Youth Specialties

"Doug Fields not only UNDERSTANDS THE NEEDS of our contemporary younger generation, but HE KNOWS GOD'S STRATEGY for reaching them with POSITIVE HELP AND HOPE."

—Dr. Bruce Larson
Copastor, The Crystal Cathedral

Too Old Too Soon

DOUG FIELDS

HARVEST HOUSE PUBLISHERS
Eugene, Oregon 97402

Other Books by Doug Fields

Congratulations; You are Gifted
Creative Dating
Creative Times With God
Creative Times With Friends
How Not To Be A Goon
If Life Is a Piece of Cake Why Am I Still Hungry?
More Creative Dating
Too Old, Too Soon

All Scripture verses in this book are taken from The Everyday Bible, New Century Version. Copyright © 1987 by Worthy Publishing, Ft. Worth, Texas 76137. Used by permission.

Published in association with the literary agency of Alive Communications, Diamond Bar, California.

TOO OLD, TOO SOON

Copyright © 1991 by Doug Fields
Published by Harvest House Publishers
Eugene, Oregon 97402

Library of Congress Cataloging-in-Publication Data

Fields, Doug
    Too old, too soon / Doug Fields.
    ISBN 0-89081-848-7
    1. Parenting—United States 2. Parent and child—United States. 3. Parenting—Religious aspects—Christianity. I. Title.
HQ755.8.F54   1991
649′.1—dc20   90-23651
                                          CIP

Contents

Dedicated to my precious daughter,
Torie Tasha Fields,
who gives me great pride in my role as "daddy"
and ignites my joy for living.
I hope you never grow too old.
I love you!

And in memory of Torie's friend,
Jordon Jennings,
whose short life is a constant reminder that
children are a gift from God.

Introduction

A happy family is but an earlier heaven.

—Sir John Bowring

When people heard that I was writing a book about children growing up too fast, a common response was, "Too old too soon—isn't that the truth!" During my time of researching and speaking on the subject, few people have disagreed with my premise while hundreds have shared their stories in support of it.

The fact is, children are being prematurely pushed to leave the passages of childhood and adolescence and rushed toward adulthood. Parents, schools, our culture, the media, and big business are all responsible for pushing kids too hard and too fast, forcing them from the innocence of childhood before their time. It's amazing to me that substantial effort isn't being exerted to slow this rush. Many people claim that little can be done about this problem since it is so ingrained in American culture. I disagree. If your home was being pounded by a raging storm, would you take precautionary measures to ensure that it didn't collapse? I know you would. This book will prepare you to fight the storm that is directed at your child.

Slowing the premature rush to adulthood in your child's life is a difficult task because it requires two rare commodities from you: time and action. But the positive results of your investment will be well worth the effort. In this book I want to build your hope for success by exposing you to the current research on the issue and by sharing with you from my many years of hands-on education experience with teenagers as well as my continuing experience as a father of young children. This mixture of my professional and personal lives has provided me with a good balance and foundation for this project.

The following pages focus on three major areas and the impact each area has on children.

The first area of focus is *you*. A parent's "good intentions" to raise extraordinary children are often the heart of the problem. Like children, adults are the victims of social pressures, and many parents have bought the message that ordinary children are passe while extraordinary children are "in."

As a parent in the '90s, you are probably older, better-educated, and wealthier than your counterparts of a generation or two ago. You may have fewer children, but you are equipped with more information and resources to prepare your child to be the best. While there is nothing wrong with wanting the best for your child, there is no substantial evidence that *pushing* your kids to be the best is good for them. Chapters 1–2 will call you to *reflection*.

The second focus of this book is the *youth culture*. I want to introduce you to some dangers within the present youth culture that many parents either are unaware of or are denying. You will see how these dangers are ripping off our kids of their innocence. Unlike some books that focus on how awful things are and what a terrible mess our culture is in, this book goes beyond the problems to present specific ideas to help you slow the rush and ease the pain for your children. Chapters 3-8 will call you to *protection*.

The third focus of this book is *parenting principles*. I'm often asked to tell parents the specific qualities their children need in a parent. Hundreds of books have been written to address this particular parental need, but this book considers only five qualities. They are so simple that you can begin practicing them today but so comprehensive that they require a lifetime of work. These five qualities are what I call the "biggies," what kids need most from significant adults. Each chapter will give you several ideas to help you make these biggies a reality in your parenting. Chapters 9–13 will call you to *action*.

The many ideas in this book will be no more than words on a page until you begin to implement them. That's when ideas turn into solutions. As with any list of ideas, not all of them will fit your particular situation exactly. But many of them will, and the others will serve as a springboard to help you find answers on your own.

My prayer as you read this book is that you will be open to being challenged to learn more about your child's world and how you can better meet his or her needs.

Whatever Happened to Childhood?

Hurry is only good for catching flies.[1]

—Russian Proverb

Chapter 1

G rowing up in a house with a huge backyard was a great benefit to my childhood. Most of the neighborhood kids wanted to play there. We seemed to spend every waking hour playing all kinds of traditional and invented games. We built forts, made swings from old tires, waged fierce wars with fruit off the trees, jumped from the fences, and played tag with cans. We played every type of ball game imaginable in my backyard stadium: baseball, kickball, smearball, football, killball, basketball, wierdball, dodgeball, wiffleball. Even the darkness couldn't stop us. We just strung up flood lights and kept playing. There was never a down time—unless, of course, I was on restriction. All this was appropriately termed "child's play."

Childhood has changed a lot in the 20 years since my backyard play days. In today's world, the options for a kid's play time have exploded. On a given Saturday a kid can watch one of a thousand rental movies, play dozens of Nintendo games, and modem his computer into electronic bulletin boards for entertainment and information, all while listening to near-perfect music from a compact disk. While these marvels of technology have brought our children many more opportunities, they have also served to isolate them from the larger world. Many kids today feel more connected to the heroes on their TV screens or computer monitors than to real people.

Hurry and Grow Up

Today's children and adolescents are growing up too fast. Usually the child has nothing to say about the accelerated pace of his growth. His inborn trustworthiness causes him to rely on adults and the surrounding society to aid him toward maturity. The problem is that we adults are always in a hurry. So we rush our children through life because we are always in a rush ourselves.

Distinct markers that once defined childhood are rapidly fading. Children who should be playing on swings are forced to deal with adult issues.

We are so busy *doing* that we no longer have time to enjoy *being*. Consequently we have little time to give to our children. Half of all American parents say they do not have enough time to spend with their families.[2] David Elkind, author of *The Hurried Child*, says that we have become a time-oriented and time-regulated society that imparts these rushed values to children. Elkind claims, "For all our technological finesse and sophisticated facade, we are a people who cannot—will not—wait."[3] We live in a world of fast food, automatic tellers, convenience stores, and impatient people honking their horns the instant the light turns green. Time has become the most priceless commodity in America. With our fax machines, high speed laptop computers, and portable telephones it seems that we can't wait for anything.

This revolution of speed and progress can rush our children to grow up, robbing them of their childhood. By forcing them to grow up too fast we place tremendous pressure on them to perform and act older than they are, which increases their stress and stunts their development. In his book *Time Wars*, Jeremy Rifkin says, "In a culture so committed to saving time we feel increasingly deprived of the very thing we value."[4] Though we may value time, we aren't spending much of it with our families. The amount of total contact parents have with their children has dropped 40 percent during the last 25 years.[5] We have become more efficient and organized with our time, thus increasing the pace of life. As a result we have become less patient, and this hurry-up attitude has diminished our respect for the passages of childhood and adolescence. Instead we should be encouraging our young people to hold onto their childhood as long as possible. If parents will loosen their grip on time, their children will have more time to express their wonder, curiosity, and enthusiasm.

Distinct markers that once defined the difference between childhood from adolescence are blurred and rapidly fading. Children who should be playing on swings are forced to deal with adult issues. It's difficult enough for adults to think and act like adults, let alone expect children who should be running and jumping to behave like adults.

Grandparents all over our country are saying, "Parenting isn't what it used to be." They're right; times have changed. Parents in the 1920s raised their children by emphasizing patriotism, loyalty to church, strict obedience, and good manners. Today's surveys reveal that parents stress independence, common sense, and sound judgment while the values of the '20s receive low ratings.[6]

Our society's shift in thinking is transforming the way we view and treat children. At one time we treated the period of childhood and adolescence as special and different, worthwhile and beneficial to the child. Now we think of it as synonymous with adulthood. These changes are affecting solid Christian families. I know too many God-fearing Christian parents who are either denying the effects of change or simply don't understand what is happening within the culture that is pushing their children toward adulthood. As a consequence of this denial and ignorance, parental responsibility is being replaced by the authority of a valueless society which soon becomes a surrogate parent. I'm sure God has major problems with this shift since he ordained that children be taught in the home by their parents (see Deuteronomy 6:7).

Today's parents must be aware of the changes within culture in order to prepare for the inevitable consequences of these changes on their children. Parents can no longer claim, "It won't happen to my children." Cultural changes are moving into all types of neighborhoods. It doesn't take a brilliant mind to notice that times are changing, but it does take a wise parent to teach, establish, and maintain values and standards during these times. No matter how fast our society changes, there are still parents who refuse to allow these changes to destroy their children and undercut their role as parents. Their commitment to understand and keep up with the changes may leave them challenged and, at times, frustrated. But their children will reap the benefits for years to come.

Those of us who are willing to accept this challenge, must take off our rose-colored glasses, face the reality of a changing culture, and pay the price. Only then will we find that it is not too late to rescue our children's childhood. First, we must become educated on our changing culture, its influence on our children, and the potential consequences of these changes. Second, we need to understand some of the attitudes in our world that are crippling the development of children. And, third, we must take action to protect, encourage, and guide our children through unique passages of childhood and adolescence.

Growing Up in a Changing World

Consequences are an inevitable aspect of change. Within our rapidly advancing culture we tend to applaud progressive developments. But we need to be careful with our praise. Not all seemingly positive discoveries and changes have beneficial consequences for you or your children. Presently, many such changes are moving us away from family values which were once deemed sacred and nonnegotiable in our culture. While some may term these advances progress, the accompanying collapse in morality threatens to destroy the family.

An example is the first contraceptive pill, which was licensed for use in 1960. This scientific breakthrough provided women with the most convenient form of birth control yet developed. It allowed for increased exploration of sexual behavior and provided women the freedom of sexual pleasure without the fear of conception. But this new liberty also had an incredible impact on the sexual revolution of the '60s, which loosened traditional values regarding the dignity of individual sexuality.

> *Change is going to happen, but we need to understand that the destruction and pain many of these changes bring isn't in God's design for the family.*

Another cultural "advance" which backfired on our children is the increase in affluence in our country. In the 20-year period between 1960 and 1980 America spent twice the amount of money on children than ever before. Yet during this same period the juvenile delinquency rate in our country doubled, drug and alcohol abuse went through the roof, abortions increased, youth homicide multiplied, and SAT scores (measuring academic performance for college-bound students) fell to their lowest levels in the history of our country. According to the federal government, the mortality rate for all age groups in the U.S. dropped during this period—except for our young people. Our kids didn't die because they lacked health care; they had some of the best care in the world. Rather they were killing themselves through suicide, drunk driving, drug overdose, and homicide.[7]

There is something wrong with a country as wealthy and opportunity-laden as ours when our kids have as many problems as they do. This is great cause for sadness.

Another example of change and consequence is the rate at which knowledge is increasing. According to some estimates, by the year 2000 the amount of knowledge the human race has accumulated will double every five weeks! But think of the consequences for our children. What they are taught at the beginning of the school year may have to be updated seven times before final exams.[8]

Granted, change is going to happen and consequences will follow, but we need to understand that the destruction and pain many of these changes bring isn't in God's design for the family. I can relate to the parent who finds it difficult to stay abreast of all the changes and influences affecting the growing child and adolescent. One of my tasks as a youth worker is to study our culture, and yet even I can't keep up with the changes. I'm in a continual state of shock over the pressures and influences facing today's children. It's really frightening to be a parent in today's world.

I have the privilege of working with and speaking to some wonderful kids. I'm allowed to share in their joys and sorrows. Unfortunately I've seen many of them damaged by our society and wounded within today's fallible family structure. I find that many young people are living in a survival mode rather than enjoying the opportunity just to be alive and young. Each year I hear more talk about stress and suicide among kids, the painful and deadly consequences of a changing world. We must allow these potential consequences to motivate us to better understand what children are facing and to take positive action steps to help our children survive the rush to adulthood.

Grown Up Attitudes

There are two harmful attitudes in our present culture that complicate the problems children face and prompt them to grow up too soon. These attitudes are encouraged and supported through culture and families, and they directly affect our parenting styles. At first these attitudes may hide themselves in the form of good intentions, but a deeper look will bring to light their danger.

Bigger Is Better, and Better Is Best

Sixteen-year-old Kady told me that she feels an incredible pressure to win every swimming event she enters. Her dad urges her, "You've got to keep our family name in the record book." This coercion pushes Kady to swim every day year round at 5:00 A.M. and after school. She doesn't even like to swim anymore, but she feels pressured to be the best so she won't let her family down.

Recently Robby and Ryan got into a fight over a silly game of bumper pool in our youth center. They started out playing for fun, but they both knew that somebody had to win. Neither guy was willing to lose, and they let the whole room know it. My reaction was, "Come on, you guys! Who gives a rip who wins this stupid game?" But as I thought about it I realized that they *both* cared who won. They were growing up in a society that pushes children to be the best in everything—and losing isn't an option.

As our society continues to highlight and emphasize accomplishment, an award-for-performance attitude is communicated loudly and clearly to our young people. They hear adults boast that bigger is better, richer is more rewarding, power buys prestige, position ensures popularity, possessions bring pleasure. These declarations leave little question in the minds of our children about America's formula for success: be the best. Play is out and competition is in. School and play activities are perceived as a series of competitive events. They are conditioned to believe that they must be the best in what they do as measured on a pass-fail basis. Alexander Astin, professor of higher education at UCLA, believes that young people are a reflection of our competitive society. He comments that students today have "raised their aspirations and want to grab a hold of anything that will increase their competitive edge."[9]

A competitive attitude can provide positive fun and healthy experiences. But often competition becomes too important and leads to destructive behavior. I'm not sure the attitude of competition is genetic and inherited or environmental and learned. But I do know that adult expectations and attitudes regarding success increase the pressure for children to grow up to be the best. I once was amazed that many eighth grade students are already worried about passing their SATs and getting into college. Now it's unbelievable but true that academic pressure is being felt by kids in kindergarten. I remember kindergarten being a time of blocks, rest time, singing songs, and playing games. Now some states require a standardized written exam as part of a "readiness assessment" to determine which students will pass and fail kindergarten. The delayed entry into first grade rose from 5 percent to 20 percent over the last ten years.[10] If a child fails this test (and depending on the school, 13-61 percent did fail), the message his failure communicates to him may have damaging, long-term effects.[11]

The pressures in life will get worse than a 90-minute test, but the longer children can be protected from competing for acceptance the better. It's tragic to think that there are five-year-olds who already feel like failures at school. They are suffering from classroom burn-out as a result of being forced into academics and pressured to learn. Within such an early stressful environment to perform and succeed children will naturally develop a must-win attitude.

Adulthood Is Better than Childhood

My parents and their peers were concerned about raising normal children. Today's parents want to raise exceptional children. This attitude concerns child development experts because of the speed at which parents and educators are pushing kids through the passages of childhood and adolescence. Children are not allowed to fully experience their primary developmental years. Parents want their kids to stay ahead of the pack, and they often look for ways to transform their ordinary children into super-kids.

> *If our kids are going to develop at their God-given pace, we must abandon the notion that they can be groomed and displayed as symbols of our proficiency as parents.*

Super-kids have their lives scheduled for them by super-parents and super-educators. An expanding market of super-kid products is flourishing because of the demand for "give my kid a head start" merchandise. Instead of allowing children to grow up at their own speed, parents feel compelled to give their children massive intellectual stimulation in hopes of growing super-thinkers. This approach to intellectual over-stimulation has been partially justified by studies with laboratory animals. Rats raised in an enriched, sensory environment have larger brains than those raised with sensory deprivation.[12] Their conclusion becomes obvious: The more input a child receives, the better. However, this theory is still being tested—on your children!

Our society has gone berserk in its attempt to hurry children into adulthood. Curriculum has been developed for unborn babies, and parents can buy special megaphones to help them communicate it. Infants are being taught to read before they are two. Parents can buy dolls typifying various adult professions with instructions for childhood vocational training in those professions. Kids are over-committed every day after school as they rush from sports activities to specialized lessons. Boys play tackle football and other competitive sports at five years of age. Children are in big demand—and make big money—as professional models. Private schools and individual tutors are commonly used to enlarge the academic potential of small children.

Sex, once only an adult privilege, is commonly talked about and experienced by children as young as 12. Kids can frequent "nudie" channels in their own homes; it has never been so easy for them to obtain pornography. Drugs are sold and used in elementary schools. High school students are acting as parents by raising younger siblings for parents who aren't at home.

These happenings may seem fictional and out of line with a child's maturity level, but they are reality. And these are only a few examples. Parents must realize that children have access to more adult experiences than ever before. The era of innocence has been lost. Kids are exposed to adult issues at a much younger age than previous generations. Forty years ago the biggest issues children faced included chewing gum and talking in class.[13] Today children's top worries include nuclear war, contracting AIDS, pregnancy, getting a good job, dying, sexually transmitted diseases, racial discrimination, violence, alcoholism, and money.[14]

Our kids shouldn't have to worry about these issues! They are being forced to deal with adult experiences and concerns long before they have developed the appropriate coping and discernment skills. Danger flags must be waved. We must recognize that children were not designed to operate on society's time clock; they run on biological time. When we allow an adult culture, filled with grown-up experiences and information, to force-feed our children, we end up with caricatures of adulthood that are over-exposed and under-developed.

Often this type of rushing is done without an understanding of the potential consequences. The push for super-kids may lead to super-problems for the child later in life. Many psychologists believe that these rushed children will become unhappy adults. They will long for the childhood they weren't allowed to enjoy because of the pressure to grow up too quickly and participate in adult activities too early. Other results may include over-dependence, feelings of being unloved, lack of purpose, lack of initiative, apathy, an early burn-out from learning, and an interference with social and emotional development.

Parents Choose to Grow and Learn

When I think about what's happening to kids in our culture, I want to fight and protect my children from growing too old too soon. Yet I must admit that I find it personally rewarding to watch my daughter succeed beyond her age-appropriate behavior. I can't deny how proud I would feel if Torie proved to be more intelligent or coordinated than others her age (which she probably is!). Her success boosts my ego, because I feel that it's proof of my excellent parenting. I get a great deal of personal satisfaction when someone says to me, "I can't believe how smart Torie is!" or "She's so cute!" or "What a personality she has!" Comments like these make me feel good about who I am.

I'm assuming that you would do anything for your children. You want the best for them, and you want them to experience the good things you never did. Unfortunately, these good intentions may be forcing wrong attitudes on your children and squeezing the precious gift of innocence from them. If our kids are going to be set free to enjoy their childhood and develop at their God-given pace, we must abandon the notion that they can be groomed and displayed as symbols of our proficiency as parents. In some cases this well-meaning push to succeed translates into a subtle form of child abuse.

There is nothing wrong with wanting the best for our children. It's a normal, healthy parental desire. But the best becomes detrimental when we push and pressure our kids excessively. When parents communicate inappropriate adult expectations children become stressed and anxious. They may perceive that their parents' love and acceptance is dependent on how well they fulfill parental expectations. Parents must be willing to allow their children to mature at their natural pace in a positive, nurturing environment. And if someone from outside the home tries to rush your children through their childhood, Dr. Benjamin Spock shares this advice: "Parents have to learn to ignore efforts to make children grow up too fast. And when other people try to rush your child into sports or reading or some other activity that you feel isn't appropriate for your child, you need to stand up to them and say, 'Go away! That's not what my child should be doing.'"[15]

Instead of preparing children to be adults we must protect them from premature adulthood.[16] This posture of protection will force us to evaluate our lives and behavior to ensure that we are not contributing to the problem. If you find yourself to be part of the problem, realize that it's never too late to change and become part of the solution.

This learned love will allow your children to mature at their own rate without having to satisfy parental demands.

I believe it's possible to raise children to be decent, moral, godly human beings in a world that seems to value these qualities less and less. In order for this to happen we must be willing to grow toward becoming better parents and learn more about children and their culture. The world isn't going to stop and wait for us to catch up in our understanding. Times, values, and norms are changing. Today's world is different from the one we grew up in. We must adapt to it and learn to nurture children in an environment that isn't as safe and secure as it once was. If we relinquish this responsibility to grow and learn, we will, as Eric Hoffer states, "find ourselves beautifully equipped to deal with a world that no longer exists."[17]

Did We Know What We Were Getting Into?

What is important today is the recognition that the family has changed....That is why everyone must assist, give aid and support to help raise the children. We have to be nurturers of all our children as a society.[1]

—Bob Keeshan
(Captain Kangaroo)

Chapter 2

December 15 is a morning I will never forget. I was filled with a mixture of emotions as my wife, Cathy, and I prepared for the delivery of our daughter, Torie. My tear ducts were working overtime. I cried for joy when the doctor explained the fetal monitor and when I heard the baby's heart beat. I cried when Cathy went to the bathroom and when she told me to relax. I even cried when someone brought me a Coke. The final outpouring came when our seven-pound nine-ounce bundle of baby finally entered the world.

As the nurses tended to Torie's needs I remember thinking, "Fields, you're a parent now. Do you understand? This isn't a dream. *You are a parent.*" I had been preparing for nine months for this moment, but somehow I'd missed the lesson on how to deal with the powerful feelings that accompanied this awesome responsibility. For years I'd been actively involved in the lives of young people as a youth leader, often pinch-hitting as a substitute parent for kids from broken or dysfunctional homes. But on

December 15 I stepped up to the plate for myself, and I was scared. It was now my full time, multi-year job to ensure the positive development of a child born into a wild and rapidly changing world. Torie must have been confused and frustrated leaving the warmth and security of the womb for such a bright, noisy, confusing, frustrating world. I had similar feelings about entering the ominous world of parenthood.

Parenting is an awesome responsibility in our fast-paced, rapidly changing society. It's so easy for our kids to get caught up in the world's attempt to rush them to adulthood. If our children are going to enjoy a fulfilling and meaningful childhood free from the pressures of growing up too soon, we must provide it for them. No one else—pastors, teachers, other relatives—can do it for us. We must shelter them from the childhood-destroying momentum of society and escort them lovingly, at their God-given pace, through childhood and adolescence.

How can we do it? In chapters 9–13 I will share with you five specific answers to that question. But here I want to provide one comprehensive response: nurture. If you will carefully and prayerfully attend to the nurturing of your child, you needn't worry about him or her growing too old too soon.

Nurture: The Privilege of Protecting

I often wish that God had designed child-raising to be as easy and as much fun as child-conceiving. Every day I'm more aware that our children and teenagers are in desperate need of guidance, protection, and nurture. This is an incredible responsibility for parents! Sometimes we are so overwhelmed by our task that we view parenting as a cross we must bear or a dreary job from which we get no days off or vacation. But parental responsibility should be viewed as a privilege. I'm convinced that our young people would benefit if we viewed our job as a heavenly appointment to empower and oversee our children's development.

Nurturing doesn't happen by accident; it's something parents do on purpose.

In his book *You and Your Child*, Chuck Swindoll refers to this privilege as a "domestic love transfer." He writes to parents:

> You are entrusted with the title deed to His property when your child is born. God gives you the children He wants you to have because of His love. . . . [They are] not the result of a mere biological process, not a financial tax deduction, not another chair at the dining room table, not an interruption in your work. Children are assigned by God, His property, delivered to you as a loving reward for you to carry on the process He began.[2]

The writer of Psalms doesn't use Swindoll's catchy phrases, but he simply says: "Children are a gift from the Lord" (127:3). If you're the parent of an angelic infant or toddler it might be easier for you to agree with this verse than if you're the parent of a rambunctious preteen or rowdy adolescent. But remember: Regardless of his age, your child needs you to give sacrificially in order to nurture his development.

What does it mean to nurture? I could articulate an academic definition or quote Webster for you, but words without personal application are empty rhetoric. Here's a question which will help you personalize the meaning of nurture in your parenting: How do you think God wants His gift (your child) to be treated? Would it help if I told you that God was so interested in your child that He was involved in forming him or her in the womb (Psalm 139:113-14)? I could beg you for 240 pages to be a nurturing parent, but I can't decide for you. I believe you know what God wants for His children (gifts). The Bible tells us: "Train a child how to live the right way. Then even when he is old, he will still live that way" (Proverbs 22:6).

You only have a fixed amount of time to invest in nurturing your child, and it should be no surprise to you that your time will go by quickly. Nurturing becomes more difficult as children grow older. Not only do they become more established in their ways, but between the ages of 10 and 15 the amount of time they spend with their families decreases by half.[3] Children whose homes are consistently characterized by parental love and caring nurture will be better equipped to resist the negative influences they will face.[4]

The Mistake of Nurture by Proxy

For several years I've had a potted fern in my office at

the church which covered the top and sides of my filing cabinet. Fortunately for the fern, I didn't have anything to do with its maintenance. A wonderful woman in our church named Barbara slipped in and out of my office unnoticed to water it, take its temperature (or whatever you do with those little soil gadgets), and prune its leaves. When I saw Barbara around the church I would thank her and remark about the plant's beauty. She always responded by saying it was her pleasure.

Barbara is no longer around, and my fern obviously misses her loving touch. It's ugly and dying (others would say it's dead, but I believe in resurrections!). I'm very aware of my fern's need for water, but I haven't put its nurture high on my priority list. Occasionally I feed it my warm, leftover cola, believing that a little nourishment is better than nothing. But my fern's only hope for health and beauty is for me to make it a priority. Its brown leaves and sickly posture are a constant reminder to me of the importance of nurture.

Unfortunately, there is no "Barbara" you can depend on to nurture your children for you. As a youth pastor I've had numbers of parents try to dump their nurturing role on me. They say things like, "Doug, would you try to fix my daughter?" or "Doug, would you mind spending a couple of hours with him and see if you can talk some sense into him?" or "Here's my child; I'll pick him up when he's 18."

It's just not that easy. Parental nurture is the unique responsibility of parents. Sunday school teachers, pastors, coaches, youth leaders, and other supportive adults may be able to help. But if you don't make the nurturing of your children your priority, your child's spirit may end up resembling my neglected fern. And parental nurture isn't a casual job. It must be top priority.

I understand that parents have busy schedules and that they also have personal needs which must be met. But when the majority of a parent's attention is diverted to priorities other than their children, they are failing in the privilege of caring for God's gift. I've watched families pay a devastating price for placing other priorities before their children. Quality nurture for you may mean delaying a few material pleasures or foregoing some attractive employment options in order to commit yourself to guiding and nurturing your children through the growing years.

This morning I lunged to catch little Torie as she slipped off the bathroom counter with her toothbrush lodged in her mouth. After safely placing her on the floor, I shuddered at the unpleasant image of her falling down face first and poking a hole in the back of her throat. But the look on Torie's face only reflected her faith in me as her father. She was smiling with confidence because she knew it was my job as her daddy to catch her.

I believe God has similar expectations of me. He not only expects me to catch Torie when she falls, but to protect her, love her, affirm her, cherish her, teach her, admonish her, and help her grow into the person He designed her to be. These acts of nurture are not only my responsibility as her dad but my privilege as a partner with God in raising her.

Growing Up without Nurture

Many children are left unwatered and uncaught falling off counters by parents and adults who either don't recognize or don't care about their God-given privilege of nurturing. This parental abandonment is characterized by schedules too busy to allow involvement in kids' lives, lack of affection, and ambiguous moral standards. Abandonment is evidenced in the children by too much freedom, not enough guidance, no knowledge of values, no discipline, and too much time at home alone.

Families eating and playing together seems to be a thing of the past. The amount of contact parents have with their children has dropped 25 percent over the last 25 years.[5] The average American father spends only two minutes a day with his children in education and communication. At this rate a six-year-old will spend more time watching television in one year than he will spend talking to his father in his lifetime.[6] Kids have very real needs, and if they don't get their needs met in an enriching home environment, they will seek to have them met by other means—often negative.

Unfortunately our world has little to offer parents in the way of nurturing assistance. Nurture in the home is frayed by an abrasive society that acts as an enemy rather than an ally. Watch the news if you need to be reminded how bad it is. Newborn babies are abandoned in trash cans, women are raped in crowded bars, and children kill their parents for life insurance money. Drug wars, racial violence, and drive-by shootings are commonplace. Murder is no longer front page news. Immorality is accelerating. We've become desensitized to the alarming. We're saddened and brokenhearted by what's happening, but nothing shocks us anymore. This deterioration in morality in society threatens the nurturing process in the home.

Our culture's acceptance of violence and evil filters down to our children. Kids hear about it, see it, live with it, and accept it as normal. As a result, an alarming number of young people are experimenting with crime, substance abuse, gangs, cults, self-destructive activities, date rape, and sexual abuse. Though we accept youth crime and violence as common, it's certainly not normal.

Thirty years ago everybody understood the importance of the family, and this high esteem helped keep many problems from entering the home. But today, though problems are more common among troubled families, pain has no boundaries. Your family is as vulnerable as the next. Some of the most messed up kids I've worked with came from wealthy families. A family's money, possessions, and status can't buy immunity from problems in this world. The healthy, nurturing nuclear family has become an endangered species.

Nurturing on Purpose

Healthy families and quality children are usually found in a nurturing home atmosphere. Cathy and I recently visited in the home of Jonathan and Crystal Holland, two kids from our youth group who have always impressed us with their positive attitudes and behavior. After spending time with their parents we understood why Jonathan and Crystal are the quality kids they are. They come from a nurturing home where the parents make the kids' growth and development a high priority.

How can parents nurture kids in this way? Someone once asked Urie Bronfenbrenner of Cornell University a similar question: What is the key ingredient in the successful development of human beings? He answered: "Someone has to be crazy about kids. Parents must make each child the most important person in their life."[7] I love that response! Bronfenbrenner may get the credit for the words, but he borrowed the concept from God.

Nurturing doesn't happen by accident; it's something parents do on purpose. I want to share with you eight forms of nurturing that are well within the capability of every parent. While this list is not exhaustive, it will help you identify some steps of nurture you need to implement in your home and affirm you for steps you have already implemented.

Nurturing through Protection

A nurturing parent seeks to protect his or her child from the influence of the world's trashy attitudes. For example, I recently talked to a father who screens the cartoons on TV so his kids are not constantly exposed to violence displayed in a humorous manner. He doesn't want his kids to think brutality and cruelty are a laughing matter. It's important enough to him that he spends several hours each week evaluating cartoons. Being a protective parent may take a lot of time.

Mike's parents didn't share this father's concern for protection. Last week I went to Mike's house to shoot baskets and help him develop a speech for his high school debate class. After playing basketball we cooled down in the backyard and talked about girls. Mike talked candidly about his struggle with lust and masturbation.

When we went into Mike's room to work on his speech I realized why Mike was having such a difficult time with lust. His walls were covered with pornographic posters. These weren't just swim suit photos; naked women were all over the place. I'm deeply concerned that any parent would allow his or her child to decorate his room in this way. This is far from being protective. Protective nurture often goes against the wishes of the children, but it guards them from dangers they're not aware of.

Nurturing through Training

Families that neglect training their children in basic life skills harm their ability to function in a healthy manner. Early childhood disciplines and manners are commonly taught in the home before children enter school. But parents often delegate higher forms of parental education—such as training in moral values—to the school system. When the responsibility of teaching right and wrong is delegated out of the home, children will likely be indoctrinated in a value-neutral or value-negative ideology where morality is relative, situational, or non-existent.

Nurturing your children requires continual reinforcement of moral values in the home. If your moral training is thorough and consistent, your children will internalize your values. Any values your kids don't learn at home will be learned elsewhere, usually from people who don't share your positive and godly values.

Sexual education is a prime example of the kind of

moral training which should happen at home. Children must learn about sexuality, God's view of sex, and the right way to treat—and be treated by—the opposite sex in the safe, loving, protective environment of the home. Neglect in this area of parental education forces kids to learn about sex from friends, on the streets, in the media, etc. No half-hearted parental training will succeed when our world is whole-heartedly committed to influencing the minds and hearts of our children.

During times of rebellion a "do-it-my-way" attitude may strike your kids. They may experiment with other values, and you will hurt inside as they suffer through periods of trial and error. But I've seen rebellious kids, who were trained well in Christian values, return to the principles they internalized from their parents' teaching and example.

Nurturing through Encouragement

Many young people grow up lacking the nurture of verbal encouragement from their parents. If your kids leave home in the morning without receiving any words of encouragement from you, chances are they won't hear any all day. Their peers don't even consider encouragement an option; it's almost a social taboo among kids to say something nice about each other. Instead most young people are skilled in the brutal act of putting each other down for no reason. These negative comments become destructive to the child's sense of who he is and his perception of his world.

> *When you communicate your love to your children through verbal encouragement, you help them develop a foundation of confidence.*

Your children must hear praise from you during their formative years. They desire and require positive feedback on who they are and what they have done. You should remind each child that he or she is an original masterpiece designed and created by God. They must understand God's love and grace is unconditional, not dependent on their performance or looks.

Words are rarely forgotten, and when negative comments are directed at a child's attitude, looks, or performance, they stick in his mind. A nurturing parent evaluates his or her words before they are spoken to make sure they will build the child's self-image. When you communicate your love to your children through verbal encouragement, you help them develop a foundation of confidence for counteracting the daily negative assaults they face in the world. (I will share more on the power of encouragement in chapter 10.)

Nurturing through Discipline

Several months ago a mother talked to me about her daughter's apathy. She complained that her daughter wouldn't follow through on simple chores. The longer we talked the easier it was for me to see that this mom had not clearly outlined any unpleasant consequences that would follow her daughter's uncompleted chores. If the girl didn't take out the trash, her mom got angry and yelled at her, but that was it.

I suggested the possibility of restricting privileges, and her face lit. She had resisted discipline because she was afraid it would ruin their mother-daughter relationship. But once she began withholding privileges for disobedience she found that her daughter was more responsive about taking out the trash and emptying the dishwasher.

Nurturing means helping young people understand that their actions have consequences. When kids display blatant disregard for people or property and show no remorse for the hurt or damage they cause, they are undisciplined. Cathy and I have teenagers in our home all the time, and I'm continually amazed at how some of them act. I watched a high school student spill a soft drink on our carpet and just sit there as it soaked in. When I finally suggested that he clean up the spill he acted shocked, as if I had asked him to paint my house.

When we fail to discipline our children we fail to prepare them for living in a world regulated by authority and rules. Lack of parental discipline also reveals a lack of parental love (Proverbs 13:24). Nurturing your child with discipline helps him define responsibility through an understanding of right and wrong. When a child isn't disciplined for doing wrong his discernment becomes blurred. He may view his wrong action as appropriate and continue doing it without feeling any responsibility for the consequences. I believe that's why the Bible says: "Sometimes people are not punished right away for the bad things they do. That makes other people want to do bad things, too" (Ecclesiastes 8:11).

Nurture through discipline guides a child in the way he should go and teaches him responsibility for moral actions.

Nurturing through Establishing Markers

Markers are clear parental guidelines or rules for a child's conduct. My in-laws established a dating marker for Cathy, deciding that she would not date until she was 16. Cathy didn't like it at the time, but she respected her parents' marker. Today both Cathy and I are grateful that her parents nurtured her by establishing a dating marker.

I have friends who established a football marker for their son. They won't allow him to play tackle football until he enters high school, even though his friends began playing at seven years old. Some parents establish television markers to control what and how much their children will watch on TV.

David Elkind uses the term "vanishing markers" to describe the progressive erosion of markers that once established rites of passage and defined borders between childhood and adolescence.[8] Children who grow up without markers are unsure of themselves and uncertain how to behave. They need their parents to establish markers for them to help them define clear patterns for living, self-discipline, and morality. Parental markers relieve a child's stress because they ensure age-appropriate behavior.

Nurturing through Valuing Individuality

Every child is different—even those we expect to be alike. My friend, Tic, has twin daughters who are exact opposites. For their ninth birthday he allowed each girl to choose her own type of party. Abby chose to buy a new dress and invite five of her closest friends to a quaint picnic in the park. Megan wanted a new baseball mitt, and she invited only boys to play in her birthday party baseball game.

Since every child is different, we must discover ways to encourage and value each child's uniqueness and individuality. Nurture doesn't force children to be someone they aren't capable of becoming or unfairly compare them with others. Rather a nurturing parent builds each child's security by adapting to his unique style and encouraging him to develop into the person God has designed him to be.

Nurturing through Providing Positive Memories

I have vivid childhood memories of both good and bad times. I don't remember any sermons I heard, but I do remember the great fun our family had on camping trips. I remember laughing hysterically when Mom tried to water ski. I can't recall exactly what my dad said when I crashed his car, but I do remember him hugging me and communicating that he still loved me. Fortunately the good memories outweigh the bad, and the praise goes to my parents. They nurtured us kids by filling our lives with happy, memorable experiences.

Our goal as parents should be to provide as many positive experiences for our children as possible. It's unrealistic to think we can keep them from all bad experiences, but we can ensure that the good experiences outnumber the bad. (I have more to say about positive memories in chapter 12.)

Nurturing through Physical Affection

From the moment your child entered the world he desired and required physical affection. Most parents smother their infants with affection, but as kids grow older parental expressions of affection seem to disappear. It's almost as if society has determined that the older children get the less they need physical affection from us. Yet our children never outgrow their need to be nurtured through loving hugs and kisses.

> *If tough, adolescent guys enjoy the close physical head locks from their weakly youth pastor, they certainly need hugs from their parents.*

I rarely see physical affection in families. For example, when I bring kids home from a week of youth camp I expect to see their moms and dads greet them with hugs and kisses. But usually the greetings are just verbal. When I ask kids if their parents express love to them through physical affection, they often say, "My dad just isn't that way" or "My mom's parents weren't very affectionate, so neither are we." I realize that adolescents give the impression that they don't need affection, but internally they crave it—just like you and I do.

I'm an affectionate person, and I love to see kids light up when I hug them; it's a beautiful sight. I even use times of rough-housing with the teenage boys to express affection. If tough, adolescent guys enjoy the close physical head locks from their weakly youth pastor, they certainly need hugs from their parents.

Positive physical touch nurtures children by communicating trust, concern, and closeness. I'm convinced that whether your family of origin was affectionate or not, you can learn to nurture your children by expressing your affection in ways appropriate to his or her sex and age.

Most of you reading this book have great kids and a good home. Nevertheless, you are probably concerned about your child's development and troubled by what you see in our world. The chapters ahead will further open your eyes to how children are being robbed of their childhood and provide ideas to help you lessen the world's negative impact on your children. I'm sure you will agree that ignorance about kids and the world they live in is anything but bliss. Just by reading this book you are giving high priority to learning more about your child's developmental years and how you can nurture him through them.

There's no question that parenting is a difficult task, especially if you are doing it alone. But there is hope for your child and for our world. No trend is irreversible. If the healthy family is ever going be a priority in society again, it must happen one family at a time. I pray that your family will start today.

Buying In
and
Looking Good

The childhood shows the man, as morning shows the day.
—Milton

Chapter 3

C hildren don't grow up to become adults. They first grow up to be "young people"—teenagers and young adults—and then jump into adulthood from there. While this transition seems perfectly logical to us, it's not traditional. The intermediate step to adulthood we call youth virtually didn't exist until the second half of the twentieth century. The youth culture is a relatively new idea, largely the product of the baby boom.

After World War II, our parents started having babies in a big way. Between 1950 and 1960 the U.S. population grew by 28 million, an 18.5 percent leap. Another 24 million Americans were on the scene by 1970.[1] Suddenly, quiet neighborhoods across the land were invaded by kids like us with our tricycles, troll dolls, and Tonka trucks.

Adults weren't quite sure what to do with all of us. We overcrowded the schools, the playgrounds, and the beaches. They created McDonalds, television, and Disneyland to feed us and entertain us. Our parents showered us with toys their parents could never afford to keep us occupied during our free time—a luxury they only enjoyed after doing their chores. Compared to our parents' rural, austere childhood, ours was plush: generous allowances, fewer chores, and much more time to spend with our friends.

Our parents lived out their childhood and adolescence working, playing, and studying with family—parents, siblings, cousins, aunts, uncles, and grandparents. We spent most of our time with friends. Our parents were at work, our brothers and sisters were with friends their age, and most of our relatives lived in other cities and states. When we became teenagers, we were the first generation to claim that our friends were more influential on us than our parents.

Our parents' culture consisted of their family, neighborhood, nationality, and faith. Our culture consisted of kids our age: a "youth culture" made up of kids who found themselves without a significant role to play in society, caught in the void between childhood and adulthood. So we created a new society out of our common need for freedom, diversion, acceptance, and significance.

Rushing into Adolescence

The conditions that created a youth culture with the first wave of baby boomers have gotten worse in the '80s and '90s. Families have fewer children, and the extended family has virtually disappeared. Parents work longer hours and spend less time with their children. Instead they place them in day care centers or allow them to come home to an empty house, meaning that today's kids spend even more time with their peers than we did. Adolescents today have more discretionary money than any previous generation. We have perpetuated and amplified the conditions that make the youth culture possible.

Although it was created to a great degree by negative circumstances—the disruption of the traditional, rural family—today's youth culture isn't all bad. It provides stability and direction, diversion and responsibility, love and acceptance for millions of young people living in homes (or on the streets) where these needs aren't being met. And even kids from good, nurturing homes are further enriched by the extra source of these qualities their friends provide.

But, unfortunately, many of the behaviors and attitudes of the youth culture *are* negative, forcing today's preteens and teens to discard childhood too early and replace it with a hollow and dangerous caricature of adulthood. Adolescents no longer wait until the magic age of 18 or 21 to sample the thrills of adulthood: sex, money, power, drugs, freedom to see, do, and say what they want.

The Downshift of Privileges and Vices

Many of the privileges and vices of adulthood are now available to teenagers. Likewise, teenage privileges and vices are now accessible to children.

Look at sex, for example. Thirty years ago children found it disgusting, teenagers learned about it, and adults did it. Today children learn about it through TV, movies, music, and school, teenagers are doing it, and many adults are disgusted with it!

Money is another privilege that has downshifted in age. Years ago children didn't care about it, teens needed it, and adults had it. Today, children are bombarded by TV ads convincing them that they need the toys only money can buy, teenagers earn heaps of it through part-time jobs and hefty allowances, and adults are in debt.

Exposure to violence comes earlier too. Once children were protected from seeing it, teenagers were permitted to watch it in horror films, and only adults actually committed it. Nowadays children see it, teenagers commit it, and adults get rich producing films and TV programs about it.

A study conducted by the Fullerton, California, Police Department and the California Department of Education reveals that the rush to adulthood has also spurred a down-shift in the kinds of discipline problems schools deal with. Kids today are dabbling in behavior our parents rarely even thought about.

Major Youth Problems

1940s	1980s
Talking in class	Drug abuse
Chewing gum in class	Alcohol abuse
Making noise	Pregnancy
Running in the hallways	Suicide
Getting out of place in line	Robbery
Wearing improper clothing	Assault
Not putting paper in waste- baskets	Burglary
	Arson
	Bombings[2]

Today teenagers don't just act like they're adults; most actually consider themselves to have arrived. A survey of 12- to 19-year-olds found that 68 percent think of themselves as adults, although only one in four is aged 18 or 19.[3]

With the downshift in privileges and vices continuing, even if your children are years away from adolescence you need to understand the youth culture. It is the future to which your children aspire. A child's immediate goal is not to grow up to be an adult; it's to be a "big kid"—an adolescent. Adulthood is too far away for him to imagine; adolescence is just around the corner.

In order to understand the youth culture you must understand four of the strongest influences on youth today. In this chapter we will consider two of them: materialism and physical appearance. In chapter 4 we will look at two more: substance abuse and sexuality.

Buying into Adulthood

Money to spend, time to spend it, and a group of peers to spend it with—today's young people are richer than ever. In 1989 America's 23 million teenagers spent $71 billion on themselves and their families,[4] a fact that doesn't go unnoticed by companies selling movies, make-up, music, and milk shakes. The teen population is growing in numbers and wealth, and these companies intend to grow with it. The youth market is big business!

Advertisers play upon teenagers' insatiable hunger for freedom, diversion, significance, and acceptance by conveying the idea that certain products will make them thin, free, happy, handsome, popular, rich, virile, sensuous, "grown up," and the envy of their friends. But if any of these products do bring happiness or acceptance, they do so only until next year's trends or technology blow them into the wasteland of nerdiness or obsolescence.

Today's youth can now afford things once considered the material rewards of adulthood. In 1980 12 percent of all driving-age teens owned their own cars; in 1990 the number jumped to 36 percent. In 1990 47 percent of all teens owned their own TVs, up from 29 percent a year earlier.[5] About 44 percent now have their own VCRs—toys that didn't even exist until the late '70s.[6]

> *Materialism is also prompted by parents who buy their children lots of toys to alleviate the guilt they feel for spending so little time with them.*

Since most parents pay for housing, food, and medical expenses, young people have few monetary responsibilities. So they invest their money in comforts and pleasures such as fast food, cassettes, CDs, movies, stereos, bikes, cars, concerts, ski trips, clothing, shoes, jewelry, and cosmetics. Those with lots of money spend more, and those with little try to keep up by working more hours or going into debt. Over half of all 16- to 19-year-olds work, some just to make car payments so they can drive to work![7]

In their quest for the freedoms and material pleasures of adulthood, young people discard the true freedoms of childhood: freedom from debt, freedom from long and tedious work hours, and the freedom to enjoy simple pleasures.

The desire for money and the thrills it can buy has seduced many teenagers into another material high: gambling. A study of 2,700 high-schoolers published in 1989 revealed that over half the students gambled at least once a year. Of those who gambled, 36 percent said they started at age 11 or younger, 13 percent financed their gambling with crimes, and 5 percent were classified as pathological gamblers. (About 1.5 percent of all adults are considered pathological gamblers, 96 percent of whom began gambling before they were 14!)[8]

Kids gamble most heavily on sporting events, cards, and lotteries, with some running up debts of hundreds and occasionally thousands of dollars. A friend of mine just returned from speaking at a church camp. He was shocked to learn that a lot of the boys in camp stayed up until 2:00 in the morning gambling. More than one of those kids came home from camp with a substantial poker debt from the summer.

It may look like the fixation with money and material possessions develops in adolescence, but it actually begins in small children. We as parents instigate a lot of it ourselves through what I call the Big Wheel syndrome. I was an adult by the time those slick, plastic three-wheelers were invented, and I envy the kids who get to race and slide around on them. I can't wait to buy one for my daughter so I can experience the thrill through her. That's the syndrome: showering our children with toys we never had in order to experience the thrill vicariously.

The rush to materialism is also prompted by parents who buy their children lots of toys to alleviate the guilt they feel for spending so little time with them or for hurting them through a failed marriage. And we are surrounded by neighbors who lavish toys on their kids, so we do the same in order not to appear stingy or unloving by comparison.

Going against the Cash Flow

Yes, materialism is rampant among American youth. But as a parent you can help prevent your children from getting hopelessly caught up in it. Since you are your kids' first and strongest role model in this area, the first place to start is with your own money habits. Here are some ideas:

Think about spending. We have friends whose children asked them, "Why don't we move to a larger house?" The couple replied, "We can afford a larger house, but we have good neighbors and strong friendships here, and these are more important to us than having a large house at this time in our lives."

If your purchase decisions are made primarily on the basis of whether or not you have the money, you are teaching your children that it's okay to buy something as long as they can afford it. Kids need to see you choosing *not* to buy things you can afford and to learn why you make such choices. Wise spending is often tied to personal and family values. Discuss buying decisions with your children by identifying the impact such a purchase will have on your spiritual life, the environment, etc.

Back off on borrowing. Many adults fall into the trap of buying more than they can afford through credit cards and no-payments-till-next-year plans. While there may be very good reasons that your credit card balance is so high, it's possible that the problem just might be your lack of discipline when it comes to spending and saving money. Even a child can see the absurdity of paying the bank 20 percent interest on credit card balance while the bank only pays you 5 percent interest on your savings. It will be difficult for you to convince your children to postpone purchases until they have the cash if you don't model the same behavior.

Save a slice. After you pay for housing, food, transportation, and health care, how much of what's left goes into a savings account instead of getting spent on "stuff"? Your children should see you saving a slice of every dollar you earn and be encouraged to do the same. If they don't develop consistent habits for saving money when they don't have any bills to pay, they will have difficulty saving anything when they have to pay to live.

Give back to God. Do you really believe that your money belongs to God and that He graciously allows you to manage it and use it? Do you regularly give a portion of your money back to Him in offerings, gifts to the needy, etc. as a way of saying thanks for the money He allows you to use? Let your children see that you take God's principles for stewardship seriously. Allow them to help you decide where your gifts will go and how much you will give.

Start a special needs fund as a family. When a child discovers a person or cause that deserves financial assistance, let him make the gift. Consider sponsoring an orphan with a monthly gift to which all family members contribute an amount they can handle. In most orphan-support programs your kids can write to and receive letters from the child they help.

Leading by example is crucial, but it's not enough. Here are some pro-active steps you can take to limit the material madness in your children and adolescents:

Think small. Parents often project onto their kids the adult perception that bigger is better. We buy them big, expensive toys, throw elaborate birthday parties, and take them to spectacular amusement parks. No wonder they grow up with an unquenchable appetite for more stuff and experiences!

But many small children are overwhelmed, frightened, and exhausted by extravagance and excess. Small, simple toys, parties, and family activities may seem inferior to you, but they're probably more fun for your kids—and better for them too.

Hide some gifts. Even if you are careful about giving too many toys to your small children on birthdays and Christmas, it's tough to control the flood of gifts from relatives. So after they have opened and played with all their gifts and their attention is directed elsewhere, box up some of the toys and stash them away for another time. Your kids will probably be so overwhelmed by the gifts you leave that they won't even miss the gifts you hide. You can "give" these gifts later when the first toys break or lose their appeal.

Another way to handle an over-abundance of gifts is to talk to your child about less fortunate children who would love to have just one of his toys. Take him to a children's hospital or orphanage and present one of his toys to a needy child (perhaps one that you gave him so another relative won't be offended).

Rotate toys. Torie had an inflatable turtle that she hadn't played with in several weeks. I put it in the closet for a few months, then brought it out the other day and gave it back to her. Her eyes lit up because to her it was a brand new gift. Old toys will seem like new to your child when they are periodically hidden and then returned to the toy bin.

Turn off the TV. Kids who watch less television "need" fewer toys because they're not bombarded with as many toy commercials that show them what they're missing. You can curb your child's appetite for goods by limiting the amount of commercial children's programming he watches. (For some creative ideas for entertaining your children without TV, see chapter 5.)

Anticipate "gimme" temptations. Just like you, your child can walk into any store and find something he wants but probably doesn't need. Before going into a store with your child, explain to him what you plan to buy and whether or not he'll be allowed to buy anything. Secure his response to make sure he understands what you expect and what the consequences will be if he starts into the "gimmes." This is a perfect time to discuss the difference between needs and wants and to train your child to resist the temptation to buy on impulse.

Go one-on-one. The mother of a four-year-old boy told me, "When he gets the 'gimme's,' I know that I haven't been spending enough time with him reading, talking, going for walks, or playing catch." Sometimes it's that simple. Like adults, kids at any age with unmet social, emotional, or spiritual needs will look for material solutions.

Rick is a student in my youth group who used to drive every adult leader crazy. He'd make every effort to get the attention he desperately craved by acting up in strange ways. At first we thought he was weird, but as time went on we realized he was crying out for attention. When my staff began to give him attention and take him seriously, we found that Rick is really a good kid, and he has become a leader in our group. Taking time to play with, listen to, and meet the needs of your children will help defuse their "need" for things.

Play toyless. Establish periods of toyless playtimes with your young children. Playing without toys forces children to use natural objects to create toys and games. My daughter has more fun playing hide and seek, chase, laundry basket race, and tickle wrestling than playing with her toys. When we're outside the house Torie and I play with stones, leaves, sticks, pebbles, and sand. Such adventures help kids understand that fun is created, not bought.

Hearing teenagers continually complain about being bored has taught me the importance of teaching young children to have fun without toys. When children rely on toys or being entertained for their fun they develop the attitude that they must have stuff to make them happy. If kids can't make fun out of nothing, you can give them the greatest toy in the world and they'll quickly grow tired of it.

The earlier your kids learn this lesson the more fun they will have as adolescents.

Reduce stockpiles. Cathy and I never realized how much stuff we owned until we packed, hauled, and unpacked it all when we moved into a new house. We wouldn't get so overloaded with life's baggage if we made a point of unloading some old stuff every time we got some new stuff.

Start a family tradition. Whenever a family member (including you) gets new toys or clothing, he has to give charity the same amount of old toys or clothing. Of course, you can make exceptions to the rule when they're justified, but they remain exceptions. You'll be amazed at how this strategy will help keep you and your children from getting attached to material goods and how much easier it will be to move.

Watch their work. When teenagers enter the work force they may settle for any job that provides them enough money to fuel their materialistic urges. Encourage your teenager not to evaluate a potential job strictly on the size of the paycheck. Help him consider how the job will effect his priorities in life: study time, family time, friendships, and future.

Depending on your family's financial situation, your child may need to work in order to buy some of his clothes, pay for car insurance, etc. But if his need isn't so great, you might suggest alternatives such as doing volunteer work for a cause he supports or working as an unpaid intern in the field he is interested in pursuing as a career.

Dressing Up Like Grown Ups

Recently a friend of mine told me a story that illustrated another strong influence of our culture which is rushing our children into adulthood. His 11-year-old niece returned home from a day at the amusement park and proudly showed her mother a poster she had made at the photo booth. It was a picture of her beautiful, innocent face mounted on the body of a voluptuous, scantily-clad woman. Her mother later told my friend, "The picture made me feel sick."

Closely tied to the cultural pressures of materialism is the strong focus on appearance. Kids have always wanted to look like adults, but I think our culture has gone overboard in helping them. I don't consider myself old-fashioned, but I have a problem with fifth-grade girls wearing makeup and shaving their legs and with third-grade boys strutting around in $100 athletic shoes. I'm uncomfortable with perfume companies concocting expensive fragrances especially for children.

Kids are spending more money on clothes and dressing up like adults younger than ever. Teenage girls spend over $5 billion annually on cosmetics and $16 billion on clothing.[9] In several cities across the country kids wearing expensive shoes, jackets, and jewelry have been robbed of their wardrobes, leading some schools to outlaw pricey duds and others to institute uniform dress codes.

The preoccupation with appearance, especially a thin one, leads many girls to drastic measures. One study showed that 13 percent of tenth-grade girls reported performing purging behavior such as self-induced vomiting and use of laxatives and diuretics.[10] The rise in bulimia and anorexia nervosa cases among adolescents is a testimony to the fact that appearance counts more than ever with kids.

Another increasingly popular appearance enhancer is cosmetic surgery. An informal survey of plastic surgeons showed that the number of teenagers going under the image knife has doubled in the past five years, and now accounts for as much as 25 percent of the plastic surgeon's business. Nose and ear jobs are the most popular, but dermabrasion, liposuction, and breast augmentation are gaining. Many Asian teens have their eyelids reshaped to appear more Caucasian, and some black youths go in for narrower noses and lips for the Michael Jackson look.[11]

It is the quest to "fit in" that causes much of the preoccupation with outward appearance during adolescence. Many parents inadvertently prime the pump much earlier. Parents who insist on dressing themselves and their children in designer clothes convey the dangerous message that wearing the right clothes makes you a better person. When kids learn from us to look for happiness in material things like clothes, we are starting them on an expensive and ultimately dissatisfying journey.

Parents pay more attention to the physical appearance of their children today than in previous generations. It's not that our parents didn't care how we looked in public, we just didn't make public appearances as often as today's kids do. We spent most of our early years at home with Mom running around in little more than fluffy slippers, cowboy hats, and Superman underwear. Many of today's kids dress up for preschool, day care, and music classes. That means kids need clothes—and lots of them. There's nothing wrong with nice clothes and a clean face, but your kids need to know that your love for them is not based on how they look or what they wear.

Guidelines for Appearance

Your children are growing up in a culture that puts physical appearance at the top of the priority list. It doesn't belong there. Here are some practical ideas you can use to help your kids develop healthy attitudes about how they look.

Let kids choose. Let your children select the clothes they'd like to wear for the day. If their choices are definitely inappropriate for the occasion, explain why. However, if they select something satisfactory but not what you would have selected, hold your tongue. A child's positive feelings about himself and his choices are far more important than how proud he makes you feel about how cute he looks.

Make room for messes. The best way to protect your kids from premature sophistication in their appearance is to constantly remind them of how much fun it is to be a kid. Let them get dirty—play in the mud, splash in the puddles, mess up their hair, go barefoot. When parents can't relax their expectations and allow their children to be messy once in a while, they send a message to their kids that their appearance is all-important—which it's not. The pressure for appearance is so strong in some kids that they grow up starving themselves (anorexia), intentionally vomiting (bulimia), and having reconstructive surgery in an attempt to look better.

Let kids pay for fashion "upgrades." Keeping your kids in decent clothes can be expensive, but it can be a financial disaster if they (especially teenagers) insist on wearing the latest fads. Offer to buy your children good, fashionable clothes. If they "must" be seen in more expensive clothes, give them the money you would have spent and let them buy their own clothes, paying the difference out of their own pockets. Young people who have to use their own money for clothes and miscellaneous extras usually take better care of their possessions.

Don't be a dud about duds. It's difficult to understand how wearing the right clothes impacts a child's sense of identity so strongly. If you and your child differ on his choices for apparel, don't make a life-and-death issue out of it. You won't solve any conflicts by insisting that your son or daughter wear clothes he or she doesn't like. Encourage dialogue about clothing issues. Compromise in this area can be okay. Save your inflexibility for issues like completing high school and saying no to drugs.

Getting High and Going All the Way

Adolescents no longer wait until the magic age of 18 or 21 to sample the thrills of adulthood.

Chapter 4

W| henever the topic of adolescence comes up in the media, it's generally connected to one of two issues: substance abuse or sex. Our teens are now experimenting with privileges and vices that once were confined to adulthood, and our impressionable preteens are mimicking teenagers in these areas. The rush to adulthood has become dangerous and deadly for our children as they dabble with tobacco, alcohol, drugs, and premarital sex.

Chemical Cures for Childhood

The American Medical Association estimates that children and teenagers spend more than $1.2 billion on tobacco products annually.[1] According to the Gallup Youth Survey, 11 percent of the nation's 13- to 15-year-olds smoke. Ninety percent of all people who smoke started before they were 21.[2]

Sales of snuff, the moist tobacco sold in tins (such as Copenhagen and Skoal), jumped 4.6 percent in 1989—the only segment of the American tobacco industry that is still growing.[3] Kids usually start "dipping" snuff before they start smoking. Dipping is seen as a "tough" thing to do. Snuff is cheap, convenient, and easy to hide.

Drinking is traditionally viewed by teens as the rite of passage into adulthood. For example, a friend of mine who did plenty of drinking as a teenager purposely got drunk on her twenty-first birthday to officially honor becoming an adult.

While alcohol is still the most popular drug among teenagers, its use is actually declining. One survey showed that the number of high school seniors who drank at least one alcoholic beverage in the previous 30 days dropped to 60 percent in 1989 from 72 percent a decade earlier.[4] The figure is still dangerously high, but it's a sign that MADD (Mothers Against Drunk Driving), SADD (Students Against Drunk Driving), and similar programs and educational efforts are making a difference.

The good news for our kids is bad news for the alcohol industry. The decline in underage drinking has resulted in lower sales. (Kids can't legally buy alcohol, but *somebody* has been buying it for them!) Brewers and distillers vehemently deny marketing their products to underage drinkers. As an Anheuser-Busch spokesman stated, "It wouldn't make sense to market to a group that can't buy our product."[5] Yet many alcohol companies are intensifying their marketing to young-but-legal drinkers by introducing light and dry beers, wine coolers, and sweet, fruity alcoholic drinks which appeal to the younger palate. And many of their ads are popular with adolescents (remember Spuds McKenzie?). Alcohol companies are working hard to establish brand loyalty among their potential customers, and many of our impressionable kids are taking the bait far too early.

The media and the marketers have a ferocious influence on our children. But their powers are declawed when we create loving, intimate family relationships.

Drug use among young people also has been declining. A survey of high school seniors showed that the number who had used marijuana in the previous 30 days dropped to 17 percent in 1989 from 37 percent ten years earlier. Cocaine use also declined from over 6 percent in 1986 to less than 3 percent in 1989.[6] Yet drugs like crack still rule the streets in low-income neighborhoods. Newer, faster acting, and more deadly variations of amphetamines, hallucinogens, and narcotics continue to attract users as young as grade school age.

Another type of chemical is gaining popularity among teens that rushes them into adulthood in a physical and permanently damaging way: anabolic steroids. These derivatives of the male hormone testosterone alter the body's chemistry and add strength and muscle bulk to kids who want to be bigger and stronger. But steroids can also play havoc with the body, causing high blood pressure, heart attacks, impotency, suspension of normal growth (kids end up stronger but shorter), and psychological problems such as aggressiveness, paranoia, and delusions.

A survey of students at six Arkansas high schools

---

showed that 11 percent of the boys admitted to trying steroids.[7] A Penn State survey of 3,400 high school boys turned up 7 percent who had tried or were presently taking steroids. An Oregon Health Sciences University survey of Portland high school football players revealed that 38 percent knew where to get the drugs.[8]

Most steroid use is motivated by the desire for better appearance. Some boys use hormones to improve their bodies the way some girls use purging behaviors to improve theirs. In the end, both sexes discover that they have damaged themselves internally in the process of enhancing their outer appearance.

Chemical Warfare

What can you do to help prevent your kids from getting involved in harmful substance use and abuse? Here are some ideas:

Just say no yourself. If you smoke, drink, or use drugs, there's a pretty good chance your children will too. If others in your family have had drug or alcohol problems, your kids are more likely to trip up in the same way. Children who have alcoholic grandparents or parents have three to four times the probability of becoming alcoholics themselves.[9]

If you use alcohol to alter your mood, to escape, or to help you cope, you'll have difficulty conveying to your children that drugs are wrong. Kids are simplistic in their thinking. To them a drug is a drug, whether it's swallowed, sniffed, smoked, or injected. You can argue about social acceptability, adult privilege, and stress reduction all you want, but if your child sees you using alcohol, tranquilizers, or any other substance as a coping device, you've lost the argument. It's obvious hypocrisy for you to forbid your child to use chemicals to combat the stress in his or her life when you are chemically dependent in your battle with stress.

Be informed. There are many good books available to help parents keep their kids off drugs and help those who have already started to get straight. Once parents move beyond the stage of thinking "my child would never do alcohol or drugs" and admit that it can happen or has already happened to their child, they are more apt to learn about it.

It wasn't until Craig and Cindy Sanders discovered that their son Sean was smoking marijuana that they took an active role in educating themselves about substance abuse. It seems like they call me every week to tell me about a new book they read and the helpful gems of information they gained from it. Perhaps they would have been more helpful to Sean had they started their research on substance abuse among teenagers before he started using.

Get involved. It wasn't until I became active with our city's substance abuse task force that I began to really understand the drug problem among our children and teens. By getting involved with a group in your city that is already fighting the battle you will be forced to deal with issues that may endanger your kids. There are many different groups meeting in your city that would love to have the additional support and energy you can add. You'll be amazed at how much you will learn about the problems facing your children when you get involved.

The Physical Road to Instant Maturity

A teenage girl told me the sad story of her first sexual experience at age 13. She was tired of hearing about sex from her friends and wanted to know what it was like for herself. So she went to a party, walked up to the cutest guy she could find, and asked him if he wanted to "do it." They went into a bedroom and in a matter of moments she knew about sex for herself. "Sex wasn't what I expected," she said, "but at least I knew what it was like and I was able to talk about it with my friends."

Over the next few years her lifestyle became very promiscuous as she continued to experiment with sex. She summarized her experience by telling me, "I know I'm still a young girl, but I feel really old."

The rush to adulthood in our culture is nowhere more evident or more devastating among our kids than in the area of sexuality. Preoccupation with drugs, alcohol, money, and appearance all take their toll, but our society's sexual fixation has visited our children and teens with a host of plagues: pregnancies, abortions, welfare-dependent mothers, pornography, child abuse, AIDS and other sexually transmitted diseases, sexual violence, homosexuality, and countless emotional and interpersonal problems in adulthood.

Our kids are getting into sex at a younger age because

our culture is obsessed with it. While standing in the super-
market checkout line, try to find a magazine cover without
sex—in word or deed—depicted or implied. You'll do only
slightly better at the paperback book display. Television is
saturated with sex: daytime dramas, talk shows, sitcoms,
music videos, adult dramas—even the news and commercials. And, of course, movies, music, and billboard advertising fill our eyes and ears with everything from sexual
innuendos to blatant depictions of illicit sexual acts and
relationships.

Our children observe that adults (who write and print
the magazines and books, and who produce the TV programs, movies, recorded music, and advertising) acknowledge sex as god—the creator of self-worth, deliverer from
insignificance, provider of happiness, fulfiller of dreams.
Is it any wonder that they adopt the belief system and
mimic the behavior of their elders?

Biological Adults

Most children reach puberty by age 13 or 14. At that
time they are physically capable of having sex and conceiv-
ing children, but their minds and emotions are still not
mature enough to handle a sexual relationship. When you
combine the physical maturity, raging hormones, and emotional intensity of adolescence with our cultural obsession
for sex, you have kids experimenting with sex to the following dangerous proportions:

- Half of American adolescents are sexually active.[10]

- Twenty-nine percent of all 15-year-old girls have had sex, up from 18 percent in 1982 and 3 percent in 1955. Eighty-one percent of all 19-year-old girls have had sex.[11]

- Nearly one-fifth of all people with AIDS are in their 20s. Since the disease can go unnoticed for up to ten years, many of these people were infected as teens.[12]

- As many as one-third of all sexually active teenagers have genital warts.[13]

- One in ten 15- to 19-year-old girls becomes pregnant each year.[14]

- Four out of ten girls will have been pregnant by the time they are 20.[15]

- One million teenage girls become pregnant in the U.S. each year. Of these, approximately 100,000 miscarry, 400,000 get abortions (26 percent of that industry's business), and 500,000 give birth—the highest birthrate among Western nations.[16] Through welfare and other assistance, the U.S. government spends $20 billion a year to support these teen mothers and their children.[17] Many of the 400,000 abortions are government subsidized.

In order to deal with the skyrocketing teen pregnancy problem, some health clinics have even experimented with paying girls a dollar for every day they're *not* pregnant.

Adopting this policy for all ten million 15- to 19-year-old girls in our country would cost $3.65 billion a year—if 100 percent effective. Of course, I'm not advocating such an outlandish scheme. But you can measure the desperation of the problem by the outrageousness of the solutions suggested.

The problems of teenage promiscuity, pregnancy, and childbirth aren't merely economic, nor even psychological. They are rooted in a child's need for love and significance. The longing for intimacy pulls many young people into sexual relationships, seeking a closeness they no longer (or never did) feel with their parents.

For a teenage girl, having a baby is the ultimate antidote for her feelings of insignificance. If her family and friends don't want her or need her, she can create a human who does. Boys may have close relationships with their parents when they are younger, but hugging, kissing, hand-holding, and showing the softer emotions are not considered mature male behaviors in our society—*except in romantic relationships*. A teenage boy with a shallow or non-existent relationship with his parents has only one other socially acceptable way to find intimacy: girls.

More than Sex Education

Your kids need to know about sex and its consequences. If they don't learn about the mechanics from you, they'll learn about them at school (both inside and outside the classroom), at church, or through experimentation. But sex is more than anatomy, physiology, and biology. Sex is about intimacy, implied permanence, significance, and purpose in a relationship between a man and a woman. We need to teach kids the concepts of sexuality as well as the mechanics of sex. Here are some ideas:

Model a loving relationship. You and your spouse should be a daily, living demonstration of biblical love and sexuality for your children. Boys tend to treat women the way their fathers treat their mothers, and girls respond to men the way their mothers respond to their fathers. When you as husband and wife treat each other with mutual respect and unselfishness, your children will be more likely to treat their dates in the same way.

Hopefully you are committed to your spouse for a lifetime and divorce is not in your vocabulary. But you should know the consequences of a couple's divorce on the sexual activity of their children. A University of Michigan professor is conducting a long-term study of a large sample of Detroit families who had children in July, 1961. The children—now adults—whose parents divorced while they were growing up were substantially more likely to get involved in premarital sex and to live with a partner before marriage. Living together occurred twice as often among the children of divorced parents than among those whose parents who stayed together. My own observations of kids in my youth group concur with these findings.

If you are a single parent, find a married couple you admire and respect who can serve as a model for your child. Recently, Susan's single mother asked if Cathy and I would meet with her and Susan once a month for dinner. After the meal Susan's mother wants to discuss marriage, relationships, and how husbands and wives should treat each other. Kids can learn a great deal about love from positive relationships.

Show love through touch. Hug your kids, and wrestle with them. Older kids are sometimes embarrassed by a parent's hug or kiss (or they just act embarrassed so their friends won't discover they like it!) But kids crave physical attention, and if you don't provide it they will seek it from someone else.

As a youth pastor I've watched hundreds of girls pass through our ministry. There have been a number of girls like Andrea who express themselves to adult male staff members in an obviously sexual manner. It's not uncommon for girls to hug men leaders during a greeting, but Andrea's hugs were long, tight, and sexual. Her actions made sense when we discovered that she never sees her father, and her step-dad doesn't give her any attention. She was lacking in affection at home, and part of her need was being filled through the affectionate hugs she gave.

Girls who have a cold relationship with their parents invariably date earlier, become physically intimate sooner, and have a low self-image. Boys with poor parental relationships are more aggressive, isolated, and preoccupied with romantic conquests. Kids need to feel loved, and they'll do whatever it takes to get that feeling. (The last five chapters of this book will give you specific ideas for helping your child feel loved.)

Let them read about it. There are many books you can buy for your kids on the subjects of love, sex, and dating, but there are only a few they will actually open. My book,

Creative Dating, is one that teenagers find entertaining and easy to read as well as informative. Try to find books for your kids that have this balance. When they develop trust in your recommendations, you may guide them into books with greater substance. Be sure to read all the books you recommend so you'll have a basis for thoughtful discussion.

The youth culture exists because young people have created a world of their own—with its own art, language, music, rituals, and social structures—to fill the void caused by the disruption of the traditional family. Instead of working to meet our kids' needs, the world has capitalized on their desires and fears by creating stuff for them to buy, ads to make them buy it, and trends to make them feel good when they have it and bad when they don't. The media and the marketers have a ferocious influence on our children.

But their powers to rush our children to adulthood are declawed when we create loving, intimate family relationships. Our kids need homes with clear teaching, room for dialogue and disagreement, justice and discipline couched in mercy, and *love no matter what.* They need parents who don't just tell them they are important but who organize the family in such a way that everyone plays a significant and fulfilling part in its survival and well-being.

It's time for us to invite our kids back into our culture—to make them intimate and important members of our families, churches, and communities, and to reappoint them to the honorable positions they held before the world got so crazy. It's a big task and one for which there are no short cuts. But there *is* hope.

Molded by the Media

If more Americans could be persuaded to carve out of their three or four hours of television viewing each day a period of five minutes at bedtime and use this time to ask their child a simple question—"How did things go today?"—and listen, the results in terms of individual families and society as a whole could, I believe, be highly salutary.[1]

—George Gallup, Jr.

Chapter 5

T oday's children and youth are as much the products of the media as they are of their parents. Because of the powerful homogenizing influence of the media, kids across the country dress, talk, dance, and eat virtually the same way. The pervasive exposure to the world's experiences and products shapes their values, behaviors, and self perceptions. But many of the messages they pick up in the media also encourage them to grow up before their time. In this chapter we will consider the three primary media influences on our children: television, music, and movies.

Growing Up in an Electronic Box

Many parents claim that the problem with television is its inaccurate portrayal of reality. But fiction and fantasy have always been accepted forms of entertainment—from the make-believe of children to the fiction of great Christian writers such as George MacDonald, C.S. Lewis, and J.R.R. Tolkien. Films, live theater, music, fables and fairy tales, and *The Far Side* distort reality to give us brief, healthy escapes from life's routines.

Yet even the most innocent diversion becomes dangerous when we spend an inordinate amount of time being diverted by it. *The Chronicles of Narnia*, by C.S. Lewis, is a collection of wonderful stories which allegorize vital Christian themes. But if you read Narnia books 20 hours a week for several years, you'll find yourself talking to dragons. Your addiction to fantasy will redefine reality in your life. That's the problem with kids and television. Viewing a few far-fetched programs on TV can be lots of fun, but they can't watch television hour after hour and day after day through childhood and adolescence without being shaped by this medium.

> *Television is not just entertaining our children; it has become their primary source of information about life.*

Children watch TV 22–25 hours per week—over three hours a day. It's their number one activity if you don't count sleeping.[2] Children 6–18 spend 15,000–16,000 hours being entertained by this one source.[3] By the time today's kids reach age 70, they will have spent seven years of their lives watching television.[4]

A Distorted Picture

But television is not just entertaining our children; it

has become their primary source of information about life. How accurately is TV representing life? Stephen Glenn, co-author of *Raising Self-Reliant Children in a Self-Indulgent World*, answers this way: "For the first time in history, a generation of young Americans is receiving its impressions about life passively from the media rather than from hands-on involvement with relevant activities. Generally, this perception of 'reality' is deficient in teaching the skills of patience, personal initiative, hard work, and deferred gratification."[5] Despite the hundreds of comedies, dramas, movies, talk shows, news programs, and game shows broadcast every week on dozens of channels, television is remarkably consistent in conveying the same distortions.

One of the distortions conveyed so consistently is that using alcohol is an important social activity. Kids receive this message by viewing 1,000–2,000 beer and wine commercials per year.[6] The good news on this front is that many groups are becoming alert to the dangers of alcohol advertising. As a result, the American Academy of Pediatrics has supported the movement to ban TV beer and wine commercials, and the National Collegiate Athletic Association has reduced the amount of television advertising time beer companies can buy during some college games. Several states are contemplating various ad restrictions and bans for alcoholic beverages.

The bad news is that, even if all alcohol commercials were banned from television, the message that advertised products and experiences can provide instant solutions to life's problems is still loud and clear in television ads. Thirsts are quenched, cravings are satisfied, aches and pains are cured, dissatisfaction is turned to fulfillment, unpopularity and boredom are resolved—all in just 30–60 seconds. American children will have been subjected to 350,000 commercials by the time they are 18.[7] About one-fourth of television programming is made up of ads. And because commercials are specifically engineered to leave the viewer with a strong and lasting impression, they provide much more than 25 percent of the impact of television on a child's life. You should be as concerned about the content of the commercials your kids watch as you are about the content of the programs these companies sponsor.

Prime Time Sex and Violence

There are approximately 20,000 implied sexual acts on television each year, nearly all of them outside of marriage.[8] The average length of time from a couple's introduction to intercourse is measured in minutes. Most sexual encounters on TV lack any reference to abstinence, self-control, responsibility, consequences, or contraception. As the director of Adolescent Sexuality Programs for the Children's Aid Society put it, "What kids learn from this is that sex is all below the waist."[9]

Sex on television also involves juveniles. Many programs portray sexual encounters between teenage characters and show grade school children kissing and going out on dates.

A new style of advertising has evolved from the look and style of MTV's music video programming. These commercials convey dozens of romantic, mysterious, sexually suggestive images that may only remotely relate to the product. When I first saw one of these commercials, I thought, *What in the world does this have to do with a pair of blue jeans?* Ron Lembo, professor of humanities at the University of California at Berkeley, describes sexual advertising this way: "The appeal is on a directly emotional level, and the potential for being dominated by the imagery is frightening."[10]

The most controversial message conveyed on the tube is that lawlessness and violence are normal, common, and appropriate methods of resolving conflict. One-third of all TV characters support themselves by committing crimes or fighting those who do.[11] Children 6–18 view 18,000 television murders annually.[12] The American Medical Association has referred to TV violence as an "environmental hazard" and has encouraged "all physicians, their families and their patients to actively oppose TV programs containing violence, as well as products and/or services sponsoring such programs."[13] Despite objections from physicians, educators, parents, and other concerned adults, 73–89 percent of all television programs over the past 20 years has contained aggressive behavior.[14]

Meanwhile, violence perpetrated by and against youth in America continues at a deadly rate. The Centers for Disease Control reports that one-fifth of the 22,000 U.S. children aged 19 and under who die each year are the victims of homicide or suicide.[15] Drug- and gang-related violence has reached epidemic proportions in our large cities. Reported incidents of rape, abuse, and racial violence among children and youth are also rising.

So why does our society continue to allow television to portray this kind of behavior? Part of the problem has been the failure of field experiments to prove *conclusively* that watching aggression and violence on television increases aggressive behavior. Many of these experiments showed a program containing violence to a classroom of kids, then observed their behavior during recess or lunch. These results are measured against the class's behavior on a different day with no television viewing and against their behavior after watching a prosocial program such as *Sesame Street* or *Mr. Rogers' Neighborhood*.

Dozens of studies like this have been performed. Some tended to show an increase in aggressive behavior; some showed no change. Some of the experiments even revealed that viewing prosocial programs resulted in increased aggressive and antisocial behavior. (So encouraging your kids only to watch "wholesome" programs might not help their conduct.)[16]

Furthermore, few studies have been performed which measure the cumulative effects of children spending thousands of hours viewing TV aggression and violence. It's difficult to study something so big. Nonetheless, some long-term studies have been conducted, and they don't put television in very positive light. Dr. Victor Strasburger of the New Mexico School of Medicine's adolescent division, a strong critic of television violence, concludes, "Although the exact nature of the impact of television is controversial, much information concerning the effects of television is known and is not controversial (except to network executives)."[17]

The researchers and television industry will continue to argue the issue, but as a parent you don't have time to wait for the results. It's time to ask some questions of your own: Will watching 18,000 murders and innumerable acts of physical brutality alter your child's view of interpersonal relationships? Will scenes of violence increase his acceptance of aggressive behavior in others or blind him to the violence that is occurring around him in real life?

The best way to protect your children from the wrong messages is to see that they are exposed to the right ones.

The acceptance of illicit sex and violence in our society cannot be wholly attributed to television. But it is naive and dangerous to assume that this medium—the most popular pastime among our children—is innocent of all charges.

The Learning Curve Is Down

By age 18 the average child will have spent about 20 percent more time sitting in front of a television than sitting at a school desk.[18] Such "dedication" takes its toll on learning. A California study of half a million public school students in grades 6–12 concluded that the more a student watches TV, the worse he or she does at school in general, regardless of the child's IQ or socio-economic level.[19] In another study, 17-year-olds who watched six or more hours of television per week scored about 10 percent lower on writing tests than those who watched only two hours per week.[20] This doesn't mean that all television programming is worthless; there are excellent programs out there with great entertainment and educational value. But kids can usually gain more from a "hands on" learning experience with a live teacher (and parent) than from sitting passively before the television set.

In the last two chapters we talked about the downshift of privileges and vices from adulthood to adolescence and childhood. Television has caused a downshift in knowledge. Information once reserved for the mature adult is now accessible to our young people on the TV screen. In his book, *The Disappearance of Childhood*, Neil Postman describes TV as "an open-admission technology to which there are no physical, economic, cognitive, or imaginative restraints. The six-year-old and the 60-year-old are equally qualified to experience what television has to offer."[21]

For example, not too many years ago ten-year-olds had no clue about sex—and somehow they lived perfectly normal lives in their ignorance. To learn about it they had to ask an adult, hunt for a rare pornographic magazine, or read about it in a novel written at a level they couldn't comprehend. But with sex so prominently displayed on television today, kids know about sex before they need to know—and even before they want to know.

In order to survive the perpetual ratings battle, TV shows must amaze, impress, and captivate viewers—or be replaced by ones that will. So many programs cover "real life" issues of which most children were once happily ignorant: sexual molestation, psychopathic shooting sprees, gang rape, racial violence, husbands who have homosexual affairs, child pornography, lesbians who adopt, gay satanists, terrorist bombings, etc. Sadly, the knowledge we most want our kids to receive seldom reaches the TV screen. According to TV critic Jeff Greenfield, "[TV shows] have moved into areas once considered untouchable in prime time; yet, the most common, most crucial area of all time—the capacity of modern men and women to love, trust, share, and provide a moral framework for children, this seems to be beyond their grasp."[22]

No one denies the existence of violence, hatred, depravity, and sexual perversion in our culture. But what price do children pay to gain this knowledge before they are able to process it maturely? Does early knowledge of sex make kids more promiscuous? Does awareness of constant hurting and killing induce more violence? Does premature exposure to the harsh realities of life cause some kids to give up hope, grow numb, live recklessly, or even take their own lives? Postman sums up this concern:

> What is the price of openness and candor? There are many answers to that question, most of which we do not know. But it is clear that if we turn over to children a vast store of powerful adult material, childhood cannot survive. By definition adulthood means mysteries solved and secrets uncovered. If from the start the children know the mysteries and the secrets, how shall we tell them apart from anyone else? [In] having access to the previously hidden fruit of adult information, they are expelled from the garden of childhood.[23]

These remarks remind me of something Jesus said. When the disciples asked Him who was the greatest in the kingdom of heaven, Jesus called a little child to stand with

Him and answered, "I tell you the truth. You must change and become like little children. If you don't do this, you will never enter the kingdom of heaven" (Matthew 18:3). There is something so sacred about childlikeness that entrance into the kingdom of heaven is impossible without it. The issue of childlikeness is so vital to kind, compassionate, forgiving Jesus that He suggested drowning anyone who causes a child to sin.

Pulling the Plug

There are too many confirmed dangers and unanswered questions about the long-term effects of excessive TV viewing to allow us to permit our children to spend their childhood staring at the screen. Here are some ideas you can try to help slow down television's attempt to rush our children toward adulthood:

Take a "telly" tally. List on a sheet of poster paper some of the false messages television often conveys (using alcohol and drugs is an important social activity, all problems can be solved instantly, casual sex is normal, lawlessness and violence are appropriate methods of resolving conflict, etc.). Then list on a second sheet the opposites for each message (alcohol and drugs are harmful, solving problems requires time and hard work, sex is to be reserved for marriage, lawlessness and violence are wrong, etc.). Tape both lists to a wall near the TV.

Gather the family for a two-hour viewing session. Explain that you'd like everyone to help you count the number of times each of the messages is conveyed or implied on the screen. After watching and tallying together, discuss the results of your survey using questions like these: Did the programs and commercials we watched convey mostly positive or negative messages? How could the negative messages we received be harmful or dangerous to us? Why are negative messages more popular than positive messages?

Complain about bad TV: If the programs coming into your home on TV are too trashy, you can do something about it. If you feel that the program violates the FCC's (Federal Communications Commission) guidelines for decency, you can send them a video tape for their review. The United States Supreme Court has established a definition for broadcast obscenity and indecency. If you can present evidence that the program is in violation, the FCC will take action and respond to you. Send your tape and a letter identifying the network and the call letters of the local station to: FCC—Chief of the Complaints and Investigation Branch, 1919 M Street N.W., Washington, DC 20554.

Limit your viewing. Let each family member select one hour (or an amount you determine) of programming he or she wants to watch during the week. The list of programs becomes the family's television viewing schedule for the week. This is a harsh measure, but if you are going take control of the television you must begin somewhere.

Teach through TV. Watch television with your children, and teach them about values by discussing what is being communicated. As you do, you'll get a better idea of what they're picking up, and they'll have an opportunity to learn your point of view on topics and issues. When you don't watch with them, you allow the media's message to be taught unchallenged.

I've used clips from TV programs to teach young people good values. I recently used a clip from a sitcom where one teenager was giving his friend a pep-talk about premarital sex. The clip served as a great introduction to a discussion about friendship and sexuality. This same type of discussion can happen in your home if you take time to watch TV with your kids.

Ban TV dinners. It's surprising how many families watch TV during dinner. Prior to the invention of the television, families talked together for hours each evening in the dining room during dinner and in the living room after dinner. When the television took its place in the living room, families still talked around the dinner table, but after-dinner conversation was replaced by TV viewing. Today, the portable TV in the dining room and the TV tray in the living room or family room have all but obliterated family conversation time. We eat our dinners while watching TV, talking to each other only between bites and during commercials.

We're so proficient at watching TV during meals that we can't seem to watch TV without eating, and it's affecting the health and fitness of our children. A Harvard study revealed that obesity in children increases 2 percent for every hour a child spends in front of the TV set. The study also found that only 10 percent of teenagers who watch an hour or less of TV a day are obese, while 20 percent of those who watch five hours or more a day are obese.[24]

In order to guard family conversation and individual health, you may want to establish guidelines such as the following: No TV during family meals or discussions; No unhealthy snacks while watching TV.

Wait for weekends. I'm aware of a few families who have chosen to put the TV in a closet on Sunday night and leave it there until the next weekend. One family told me that it was difficult for them to get used to weekday life without TV. But they found themselves reading, studying, and talking as a family more often. They also found that the best time to initiate a weekend-only plan was during the summer before the new fall shows came out.

Revert to radio. Your parents can probably remember the days before television when radio dramas and comedies ruled the evening airwaves: "The Lone Ranger," "The Green Hornet," "Dragnet," "The Jack Benny Show." You can still catch reruns of these classic radio broadcasts in many cities across the country. And there are other good, clean, entertaining programs available on radio to those who will search for them. Part of the attraction of radio lies in the fact that your imagination must be involved, so you become an active part of the story. Try replacing some TV programs with good radio programs.

Tell stories. Many of us grew up listening to our parents and grandparents read or tell stories to us, and we remember those stories of so long ago. Story-telling is one of the oldest forms of entertainment in most cultures. Consider replacing some of your family TV time with a story time, allowing different family members to be responsible for reading or telling a story everyone would enjoy.

Get rid of it. Some perfectly normal families I know have decided to sell or give away all their TVs. They realized that they would be healthier, closer, and less caught up in the material world if they spent their free time talking together and playing together instead of watching TV. The parents figured that their children would be happier if they learned how to create their own entertainment and smarter if they spent more time reading and creating than sitting and watching.

You may also want to consider trading in your TV and VCR for a combination video monitor/VCR unit. These compact devices have no tuner, so they can't be used to pick up regular TV broadcasts. Instead, you can bring it out of the closet when you want to watch a home video or a rented movie.

Music for the Masses

After television, popular music is the most influential medium on for our youth. And like TV, music groups and record companies are competing for the attention and dollars of our kids, and they are doing it by exploiting the same themes: sex, violence, drugs, lawlessness, and hatred, among others.

These themes are even found in the names of many bands, as an informal inventory in 1990 revealed. At least

13 bands were named after male genitals, four after sperm, eight after abortion, and one after a vaginal infection. Ten bands were named for various sex acts, eight using the "F-word." The names of 24 bands referred disparagingly to blacks, the disabled, or homosexuals.[25]

Sex, drugs, and violence are common themes in the song lyrics of many popular bands. One band sings about "niggers" and "faggots." Another sings about the joys of raping a girl with a flashlight. Another glamorizes crack-dealing and killing police officers.[26] Yet another popular band sings about damaging a girl's vagina during sex, and forcing anal sex on a girl and making her lick excrement—not exactly the kinds of lyrics you want your fifth-grader singing to himself as he mows the lawn!

The most influential music innovation of the '80s was MTV, combining the two most powerful forms of communicating to youth: television and music. MTV is watched by more than 20 million people per week, mostly 11- to 24-year-olds.[27] The popularity of MTV, together with its extensive use of emotional and sensual imagery in music videos and commercials, has prompted the American Academy of Pediatrics to speak out: "Music videos may represent a new art form, but we believe it is one that contains an excess of sexism, violence, substance abuse, suicides, and sexual behavior."[28]

Facing the Music

As a parent concerned about decency in the media, you may find it more difficult to argue against sex and violence in music than in television. Musicians and record producers are quicker to claim that music is art and not subject to censorship. They can also get away with more because albums and concert tickets are paid for directly by their fans. In contrast, TV is free to the viewer while advertisers pay the costs of programming—and receive the wrath of decent citizens if the shows they sponsor are unacceptable.

In order to combat the negative influences some kinds of music may have on your children, you must pay attention to what they listen to and take steps to neutralize those influences that conflict with family values. Here are a few suggestions:

Talk about the lyrics. If you're concerned about the content of an album your child buys, sit down together with the lyrics sheet and listen to the songs. Talk about the messages conveyed and what dangers there might be in listening to them.

Offer positive alternatives. There are a number of excellent Christian musicians today producing good music in just about any style your children might like: rap, heavy metal, pop, '50s, etc. Encourage the development of their taste in Christian music by buying them albums and taking them to concerts by their favorite artists.

Ask, don't attack. Nearly every time I come down on a song, musician, or band in front of a student, he fights back. More than any other medium, music is a part of a child's identity, and he treats our criticism as a personal attack.

I've finally learned to stay off the war path and simply ask kids what they think about a song or music group I'm concerned about. The discussion that follows is far more productive. I learn about the band or music from the kids, and they find out that I really care about their world and that I'm not out to burn their records or turn them into elevator music groupies.

Don't get personal. Music tastes are personal, and your child may have different tastes than yours. After all, did your parents like the music you listened to? If you have a problem with your child's music, figure out what you don't like about it. If your complaint is style rather than content, be flexible. Save your ammunition for lyrics that clearly violate biblical or family values.

Growing Up on the Movies

Virtually all the complaints against television can also be made against movies. But at least a movie's ticket price puts an economic limitation on the medium that television doesn't have. Movie viewing by children and adolescents is easier to regulate—unless you have HBO or Cinemax, in which case you're getting the worst of both worlds.

Most films are actually created for the youth market—preadolescent to college age. That's why the bulk of all films are released during the summer and Christmas break when students can attend them every night of the week. It's not surprising then that most films include healthy doses of the themes that appeal to youth. Sex is big in the movies, especially situations that show kids having their first experience. Violence is always a hit, as is the destruction of property. Rejection of authority is another popular theme, especially when the movie portrays kids as sophisticated and adults as bumbling buffoons.

According to the above formula, *Ferris Bueller's Day Off* was the ultimate youth film. It was weak on sex but made up for it with classic examples of the other themes. Teenaged Ferris ditches school, lies to his parents about it, and gets away with it, making several adults look ridiculous in the process. The school principal gets punched out by Ferris's sister and chewed on by his dog. An expensive car is utterly destroyed.

While TV programs feature all these themes, movies deliver them in industrial strength doses. On TV a couple's sexual activity is largely left to your imagination, but many movies show them undressing and jumping into bed. A TV character may use "clean" expletives, but her movie counterpart will use full-blown profanity, usually with God's name interjected for maximum impact. The movies are usually more explicit about the use of obscene language and sexual innuendo by children and teenagers, implying that such a level of "sophistication" for kids is normal.

Monitoring the Movies

Here are a few ideas to help you limit the negative effects of the movies on your children:

See it first. If you have serious concerns about a film your child wants to see, preview it yourself. If you think it's inappropriate, you can clearly explain why. If your child does see it, you can discuss the contents more intelligently. You may even want to form a movie preview network with other parents who share your values, taking turns previewing different movies so no one has to see them all.

See it last. Although you lose the excitement of the big screen, spilled soft drinks, and overpriced popcorn, by waiting for a film to come out on video you can preview it or watch it with your children in your own home. Watching movies on the VCR allows you to fast-forward through inappropriate scenes or stop the tape to discuss situations portrayed and answer questions.

Considering the deluge of negative messages conveyed by media, it's easy to develop an isolationist mentality: Get rid of the TV, unplug the stereo, and forbid the kids from going to the movies. But that isn't the answer.

The best way to protect your children from the wrong messages is to see that they are exposed to the right ones. And if the medium they favor is so pervasive as to drown out the right message, then you can take steps to defuse it. I know it's not easy; I wish it was!

Hurry Up and Learn

The aim of education should be to teach us rather how to think than what to think—rather to improve our minds, so as to enable us to think for ourselves, than to load the memory with the thoughts of other men.

—James Beattie

Chapter 6

When our daughter, Torie, was 13 months old, I trained her to answer the question "Who loves you?" with "Daddy." She learned well. Whenever I asked her, "Who loves you, Torie?" she lifted my spirits by responding clearly, "Daddy." Our friends thought her response was cute, and, of course, I thought Torie was bright enough to be the next Einstein!

But I soon discovered a glitch in Torie's learning. She not only answered "Daddy" to "Who loves you?" but to any other question or statement with the word "love" in it. When her grandmother said, "Torie, I love you," Torie would say, "Daddy." At Sunday school when she heard, "God loves you," Torie blurted out, "Daddy!"

A second "trick" I taught her was the answer to another egotistical question. I'd ask, "Torie, who's Daddy's little girl?" and Torie would answer with great enthusiasm and a smile, "Me!" Again I was proud. But soon she began mixing her answers. When I asked her, "Who loves you?" instead of saying "Daddy" she'd shout, "Me!"

I wish all our problems with educating our children were as humorous and uncomplicated as this. But the educational system our children are growing up in is anything but a laughing matter. We are rushing our children to adulthood today by cramming their little minds so full and so fast that we scarcely allow them room to think like kids. If we are going to guard our children from growing up too soon, we parents must act as a buffer between them and the educational system that is pushing them all to be Einsteins.

Whatever Happened to the Country Schoolhouse?

Most of us were educated in a far different manner than our parents and grandparents. Our grandmas and grandpas, and even some of our moms and dads, were raised primarily in rural communities and educated in small schoolhouses with several grades studying in the same classroom. Some of our grandparents and parents even passed through all 12 grades in the same room: the old one-room schoolhouse.

Classes in those days weren't crowded. Teachers had the freedom to allow students to progress at their own rate. Older students were responsible for tutoring younger students, and both groups benefited from the experience. Students of all ages grew up together, played together, and learned together in an atmosphere more like a large family than an institution.

An Explosion of Growth

Then after World War II, *boom!*—we were born. As we

prepared to head off to first grade, the schools had to figure out what to do with us all. This baby boom generation took the school system by surprise in 1951. In one year the school's enrollment increased by 500 percent. Our schools weren't prepared for the 4.2 million first graders who were looking for a spot in class. Stephen Glenn and Jane Nelson write, "In an hour's time on that first day of school, those children forced a total change in the system. Overnight educators threw together what was later described as 'a maladaptive response to a crisis situation,' and called it public education."[1]

This was the beginning of a downward spiral in education. The rural schoolhouses of our parents' and grandparents' day didn't work anymore. They were too small, there were too few of them, and they were too far away from the cities and suburbs to which Americans flocked in the '40s and '50s. New schools were built, and most of us were lumped into a classroom with 35 other confused first-graders.

Gone were our opportunities for individual teacher attention, student tutors, and the liberty to learn at our own pace. These advantages were replaced by a cookie-cutter approach to educating children that is still the model for most schools today. This assembly-line education has shifted the emphasis from the individual learner to the measurable components of his education: math, reading skills, scores on standardized tests, and grade point average.

In the rural schoolhouse, the emphasis was on mastering skills and demonstrating knowledge through oral recitation and written essays and reports. In the assembly-line classroom, the emphasis is on recalling recently learned information by identifying it on true-false and multiple choice tests.

The small class size of the rural schoolhouse provided ample opportunity for a teacher to dialogue with and get to know each student—his strengths, his weaknesses, his individual style of learning. But the teacher in an assembly-line classroom has too many students to pour too much time into any one of them. It has been estimated that in a normal classroom setting each student has approximately 40 seconds per hour to interact with the teacher.[2] If this is true, and one student speaks for two minutes, then four other children will miss their opportunity for meaningful dialogue.

The schoolhouse also allowed positive interaction between older and younger children. Tutoring provided the older children with a sense of responsibility and fulfillment which helped mold their identity. In today's schools we isolate children by ages and grades, giving them little opportunity to associate with anyone who is not a peer.

The results of these changes over a 40-year period have been devastating. Test scores have plummeted, drop-out rates have increased, growing numbers of children have lost interest in education, discipline problems have escalated, and tenure among teachers has fallen. Studies show that children today are observably less mature and more vulnerable in the areas of moral and ethical development, critical thinking, and judgmental maturity than students of earlier decades.[3]

Too Much Too Soon

Our children are being rushed through childhood to acquire the maximum amount of knowledge in the minimum

---

amount of time. Among parents of children age three or younger, education is the biggest concern for their children's future.[4] Formal education—reading, writing, math, and language—is even available to very young children. Glenn Doman, author of *How to Multiply Your Baby's Intelligence*, boasts that his methods allow kids to speak Japanese and English and solve junior-high-level mathematics problems by age five.[5]

Why the big rush to get such a head start on a child's education? There are many reasons. Parenting magazines and a plethora of how-to books bombard parents with information about their child's intelligence and what they can do to increase it. Day care needs force many working parents to enroll their preschoolers in classes. Societal pressures urge parents to think through and conform to the early education trend. Finally, career-oriented couples are becoming parents later in life, transferring their already-strong orientation into their parenting.

Whatever the reason, loads of parents are pushing their children harder to learn earlier. Studies reveal that the parents with the highest expectations tend to be perfectionists, controlling and critical of their children.[6] It may surprise you that there is no evidence that pushing kids into early academic achievement results in increased abilities later on. Rather, it may have the opposite effect: creating stressed out, burned up kids whose childhood has been cut short by academic demands.

Teaching for Measurable Results

In today's schools classes are crowded, time is short, and most teachers must resort to the lecture method just to get through the curriculum. As a result, objective testing is the prime method for determining a student's knowledge. The child either knows the material or he doesn't, and if he does he should be able to recognize it on a multiple choice test. Therefore, if he circles the correct answer or fills in the blank with the right word, he obviously understands the material. On this basis he is given a numerical score which indicates his status in class. This ranking distinguishes the A students from the C students and helps the teacher direct his affirmation toward students with the best scores.

But is cognitive performance on an objective test a valid measurement for whether a child has learned? Parents seem to like it because test results have become measurable ways for them to determine the intelligence of their child. Harvard pediatrician T. Berry Brazelton states, "Cognitive performance is easy to measure and to demonstrate to your friends. It becomes a way for young parents to feel successful in their parenting."[7]

Furthermore, school administrators seem to like it because it gives them a device for comparing their districts with other districts. School officials love to read headlines like, "Local school district ranks highest in math scores." This ambition can find its way into the classroom when teachers are pressured to design curriculum around the standardized tests instead of teaching the material comprehensively.

In reality, grades don't accurately measure knowledge because some students are better at taking tests than others. And those who are skilled at cramming and recalling for exams don't necessarily internalize and personalize the data. During college, my wife and I took some classes together in which she obviously had a better understanding of the lectured data. During our study sessions together I was embarrassed by how much more she understood. But I always did better on the tests than she did. My grades were higher, but we both knew that her knowledge was much more substantial.

Educators love to hear their students recite the right answers. But some teachers don't realize that students can arrive at the right answers without understanding what those answers mean. A kid in my youth group can correctly answer most Bible discussion questions by saying, "Jesus," "servanthood," "love one another," or "because God wants it that way." But many of them are far from understanding how those answers are supposed to flesh-out in their lives. When education forces and affirms memorization, our children will grow up without knowing how to ask questions. We must teach our children to ask questions and respectfully challenge teachers.

We must help our kids survive reality by teaching them to think and search for right answers.

I am an adjunct professor at a local college. When I first started teaching I was shocked at how many students wrote down every word I said so they would be prepared for the test—regardless of whether or not they understood what they were writing down. Now during many of my lectures I will purposely misrepresent and distort some of the material in hopes that the students will question me about it. In addition, I don't allow students to take notes until they can prove to me through dialogue that they understand what they're writing down.

It might be easier to live in a world where all the answers to life were clear and objective. But since life is a subjective as well as an objective experience, we must help our kids survive reality by teaching them to think and search for right answers. The educational system is off center when "such abstractions as a child's inquisitiveness, his wonder at nature, his excitement with learning, and his personality become secondary considerations to the more quantified abilities of reading, writing, and arithmetic."[8]

Launching into College

Our educational system's preoccupation with objective testing is nowhere more apparent than in college entrance requirements. Admission into college wasn't always so dependent on transcripts, GPAs, SATs, and letters from alumni. Here's what it took to get into Harvard University when it first opened:

1. When any scholar is able to read Tully or such like classical Latin author *ex tempore*, and to make and speak true Latin in verse and prose . . . and decline perfectly the paradigms of nouns and verbs in the Greek tongue, then may he be admitted into the college, nor shall any claim admission before such qualifications.

2. Every one shall consider the main end of his life and studies, to know God and Jesus Christ which is eternal life.[9]

Today's entrance requirements don't focus on the application and demonstration of knowledge but on high SAT scores, reinforcing the objective measurement of knowledge. The pressure for high scores forces some young people to retake the SAT several times in an attempt to improve their scores. Many kids labor through PSATs (Preparation for SAT) and spend hundreds of dollars on classes and computer software to help them achieve better scores. But even after all this time and effort, they may come away from their educational experience without knowing how to think for themselves.

Helping Your Child to a Healthy Education

After reading the previous paragraphs you may be ready to pull your children out of the school system and home-school them yourself. My purpose is not to make a case for or against home school, Christian school, private school, or public school. In reality, no matter which path you choose you can't completely isolate your children from society's pressure to study harder, learn faster, and succeed sooner. Rather I want to share a few ideas you can use to help slow the educational rush to adulthood your children feel in this culture.

Show love and approval regardless of grades. The day report cards arrive at home can be very stressful for many kids.

They are afraid of their parents' response to their grades. A 12-year-old recently told me that he received five *A*'s, one *B*, and one *C* on his report card. His parents focused on the *B* and the *C* and never acknowledged his *A*'s. They said to him, "If you would have concentrated more and exercised better study habits, you could have made straight A's." The kid was devastated. He had worked hard all semester and all his parents could do was criticize him for not working harder. Imagine what their response communicated to his young mind?

I'm not saying that grades are unimportant. But when your child's grades are so important that you withhold love and approval from him when they're not what you hoped for, you are fostering a damaging performance-for-reward attitude in your child that may plague him for life. We love our children because they're our children, not because they're on the honor roll.

Giving money for good grades is another subtle way of overstressing performance. When you give a child a dollar for every *A* on his report card, he will become more interested in the grade and the dollar than in learning. Rather, we must look for ways to encourage different kinds of learning (not just cram and recall) and place higher priority on building a child's identity by loving him unconditionally. (Unconditional love is discussed in depth in chapter 13.)

Value knowledge over grades. Grading is often subjective. Receiving a *C* in Mr. Smith's class may be equivalent to getting an *A* from Mrs. Jones. When parents show concern for their child's knowledge and devalue the importance of the letter grades he receives, they model positive priorities.

I worked my tail off for good grades in college, forsaking several important social and family experiences along the way, which I now regret. Even though I graduated at the top of my class, I learned an important lesson soon afterward: Few people seem to care about grades. I was crushed. I had worked so hard. When I applied for jobs, prospective employers didn't care about my grade point average, just how much experience I'd had. (I realize, however, that many technical and professional people are recruited on the basis of their GPA.) When I was asked to speak to groups, no one asked if I was *summa* or *magna cum laude*. They just wanted to know if I could keep an audience awake. Even when I went on to teach at the college level, administrators were more concerned about my ability to teach than my grades. My experience convinces me that there is little lasting value for a high GPA.

You may be thinking, "Nice theory, but everyone knows good grades get kids into good colleges." This may be true. The problem is that many parents start pressuring their kids for grades when they are still in elementary school. I've never heard of elementary grades deterring a high school senior from college acceptance. But I have seen kids so pressured for grades while at home that they were burned out by age 18 and rebelled by not fulfilling their parents' dream of going to college.

My wife didn't get good grades in high school. There was a strong priority in her home for total development. Grades weren't a big issue. After graduation she entered a junior college and gained a new appreciation for learning.

She developed her own desire to learn. She went from the junior college to a state university and completed her Bachelor of Science degree in just four years. Hers is a very common story. If kids want to grow and mature in their learning, they will—in their own time.

Teach kids to ask questions. Asking children good questions helps kids learn to think. Questions give them opportunities to ponder meaningful and important issues. Questions encourage dialogue, which increases learning. Questions allow children to process and own issues rather than merely accept them without thought.

When students ask questions they open themselves to dialogue and collaboration, which form the foundation for moral and ethical development, critical thinking, judgmental maturity, and teaching effectiveness.[10]

When children learn to ask questions they also learn to respectfully question authority, which can be a positive experience for them. I'm not encouraging anarchy but rather giving kids the opportunity to express themselves and what they believe. Just because someone is an authority doesn't mean he or she is always right or should never be challenged by young people. If kids aren't allowed to express their feelings and disagree respectfully, they will find some way to rebel to ensure that they are heard. They will develop argumentative skills and use them. But if kids are allowed to use these skills in a positive and inviting forum, the expression of their views can be a good experience.

Kids are crying out to be heard and given some validity for their opinions. Asking them questions and teaching them how to ask questions allows them the platform they need.

Search for model educators and learn from them. I recently visited with Gene Bedley, a distinguished elementary school principal who has received many awards in education including National Educator of the Year and National Principal of the Year. As I sat in Mr. Bedley's office I not only heard about his positive approach to education, I observed it. He makes school and learning fun. Children don't fear being called into his office; it's where they want to be. He studies classroom photos so he can call each one of his 750 students by name. His office is filled with plaques and sayings that reflect positive values. He requires his teachers to emphasize these values throughout the year.

Mr. Bedley's staff reflects his enthusiastic attitude, and they are obviously proud to be working closely with him. One teacher likened her job to working at a private school, only for public school pay! The parents I talked to felt privileged to have their children at Mr. Bedley's school.

As a parent, you should be looking for men and women in your community like Mr. Bedley who contribute to education in a positive manner. We need to learn from people who are doing good work with children and hold them up to other educators who can learn from their example.

Get involved in the learning. Much effort has gone into improving schools by giving them more money, better teachers, and updated resources. But educators believe we need to focus on a more basic approach to improvement:

having parents involved in their children's education. Survey results indicate that very few parents actually take time to learn with their children.[11] Tragically, parents become even less involved during the middle grades when classes and schedules become more complex and confusing and kids need their parents the most. Surveys reveal that the average mother spends less than ten minutes a day actually doing something educational with her child.[12]

Parents who are interested in knowing what is being taught at school should study their child's textbooks. I know of one family who takes time during the week to have "family study time" when the entire family studies together. Mom and Dad will either study their children's material or something of personal interest. As the parents study *with* their children they model the importance of learning.

Encourage teachers. I wish I knew by name all the teachers my children are going to have during their school years. I'd begin encouraging them all right now. Teachers spend more time with our children during the day than we do. They have the difficult and frustrating job of playing parent, nurse, policeman, and social worker to our children in addition to teaching them. Teachers need to be encouraged and built up so they can continue to inspire and give of themselves to our children. Give them positive comments and thoughtful tokens of appreciation for their efforts.

It's important that our teachers know that they are making a difference in this world. Their salaries don't do justice to their effort and value; the pay structure for teachers is ridiculous in comparison to the importance of their profession. While we can't care for teachers financially, we can give them an emotional and spiritual "raise" by meeting their basic needs to be loved and appreciated.

Chances are good that your child's teacher isn't receiving many positive comments from her students. Without praise teachers become bitter and burn out. But with praise and support from you they will be empowered to influence and inspire your children.

Provide real-life learning opportunities. Everyday life provides many opportunities for your kids to learn from you. Some of the best teaching you can do will come from the "curriculum" of daily experiences. When the grocery checker gives you the wrong amount of change at the store and you return it, you have an opportunity to teach a lesson on honesty. When your family stops to help someone in need, your child learns about servanthood. When you allow your child to help you pump gas and deliver the money to the attendant, you teach responsibility. God has given us this incredible playground called Earth to enjoy and to use in teaching our children. The opportunities are many and their applications can be life-lasting.

Your role as a parent provides you with the opportunity to be a great teacher.

I recently rented the video *Uncle Buck*. One of the scenes is a confrontation between a school principal and the title character, Uncle Buck. The topic was Uncle Buck's niece, for whom he was caring while her parents were out of town. The conversation went like this:

> Principal: I see a bad egg when I look at your niece. She is a twiddler, a dreamer, a silly-heart, and a jabber-box. And, frankly, I don't think she takes a thing in her life or her career as a student seriously.
>
> Uncle: But, she's only six.
>
> Principal: That's not a valid excuse. I hear that everyday and I dismiss it.
>
> Uncle: I don't think I want to know a six-year-old who isn't a dreamer or a silly-heart, and I sure don't want to know one who takes their student career seriously.

We need this type of concern from people who are willing to stand up for children and ease the pressure of an assembly-line, reward-for-performance educational system. Our kids need to learn to think and be taught at a pace that is comfortable and common to their maturity.

Successful education must begin in the home. Don't sell yourself short. Your role as a parent provides you with the opportunity to be a great teacher. I like how Bruno Bettelheim describes what parental influence should be: "Since the future is always uncertain, we cannot know what particular problems our child will encounter in life; therefore the best we can give him on his way into life is our trust in him and a sense of his own great worth."[13] And I might add—an unswerving love for the Lord. . . .

Growing Up Alone

If we continue to dismantle our American family at the accelerating pace we have been doing so since 1965, there will not be a single American family left by the year 2008.[1]

—Amitai Etzioni

Chapter 7

J osh, a student in my youth group, lives two different lives. His parents are divorced, so Josh lives with his mother one week and with his father the next. His room at his mom's house is tidy. His other room is cluttered and loaded with sports junk. Since each parent disciplines him differently, Josh is constantly adapting. He tried to explain to me the difficulties: "It's a lot of work to live with two sets of parents—more than I like sometimes. My mom makes me go to bed at 9 PM, but my dad allows me to stay up until 11. My mom lets me snack, but my dad never has any food in the house. I can watch whatever I want on TV when I'm home with Dad, but Mom only lets me watch one hour a night. It's that kind of stuff that makes my life confusing."

Josh's experience reflects another characteristic of our culture that is robbing our kids of their childhood: the disintegration of the traditional family. This is the most difficult chapter I have had to write. I kept putting it off because I don't like to be reminded of the pain associated with kids growing up in broken homes or homes where both parents work long hours. When kids grow up experiencing limited interaction with their parents, it results in pain for both.

Who's Minding the Kids?

Everywhere you look today families are falling apart, parents are working long hours, children are left home unsupervised, and their unlimited freedom provides them with unlimited opportunities to grow up too fast. The days of Ozzie and Harriet and the Cleavers representing the typical American family are gone. Consider some of the current trends and projections:

- At current rates, half of all marriages begun in the early 1990s will end in divorce.

- Half of the young children alive today will spend at least some time in a single-parent family before the age of 18.

- There is a substantial decline in the standard of living of divorced women with children.

- Because 75 percent of those who divorce eventually remarry, an increasing proportion of children will grow up with step-parents and step-siblings.

- Over 50 percent of mothers with preschool children work outside the home, as do 73 percent of mothers with school-age kids.

- Only 7 percent of school-age children live in a two-parent household where there is only one wage earner.[2]

I grew up in what was once considered a normal, traditional family. My dad worked hard at his job while my mother (who claims she worked harder!) stayed home to take care of three children and tend to the needs of the house. There were 15 homes on our block, and all but one maintained this type of lifestyle.

But in today's world, the traditional family is in the minority, accounting for less than 7 percent of America's population.[3] Divorce and dual-income families are the primary reasons that many children grow up virtually alone.

These parents are caught. Their children are the victims of their absence.

It's generally accepted as normal in our culture for children to spend a great deal of time at home without their parents. I recently saw several Hallmark greeting cards designed especially for parents to give to children who are left home alone for part of the day. These cards are supposedly the next best thing to a parent being there in person. For example, a child begins his day waking up to a smiling elephant card from his single mother who has to leave for work early. The card reminds him not to forget his lunch and to have a super day at school.

Most parents hate the results of these family circumstances. Divorced parents didn't intend to bring children into the world only to rip their lives apart because they couldn't solve their marriage difficulties. And couples in economic predicaments requiring two incomes don't like their situation any better. These parents are caught. Their children are the victims of their absence. This absenteeism obviously makes nurturing the children more problematic and drives children to be more susceptible to daily peer and cultural temptations.

Let's take a closer look at why so many children are growing up with such limited interaction with one or both parents.

Single-parent Families

I was recently driving home from a camping trip with a van full of ninth-grade students. Jeff and I began talking about his parents' divorce, and within minutes everybody in the van was chipping in his or her feelings and opinions about divorce. They had a lot to say—11 of the 14 kids came from broken families. Most of the kids I work with either live or have lived in a single parent family.

Roughly one-fourth (24.3 percent) of today's children live in single-parent families. That's double the number from 1970 (11.9 percent).[4] Twelve and one-half million children under the age of 18 live with only one parent.[5] Though these numbers are staggering, they really don't mean much until you step through the front door of a single-parent home and share in their pain. My heart breaks for these struggling families. It's hard enough for two parents to raise kids, let alone a single parent. The kids lose out on so much nurturing, and the parent(s) struggles just to do his or her best.

My friend Linda has three children, ages four, nine, and twelve. Every morning she makes sure they are bathed, dressed, and fed, and then hopes they don't kill each other while she hustles to get ready for work. At 7:45 AM she races off to get her two older kids to school, drop her four-year-old off at day care, and commute 25 miles to work by 8:30. After a strenuous nine-hour work day she returns home to cook for, play with, bathe, tutor, and referee her kids until bedtime. By 9:30 she finally has time to read the paper, watch the news, and pay the bills before retiring for the night, only to start the cycle again six hours later. She is often physically exhausted, mentally drained, and emotionally spent—and I can't blame her.

Children in single-parent families tend to feel neglected, ripped-off, depressed, and abandoned. These are tough feelings for a child to deal with in a situation over which he has no control.

Fast-track Parents

Even when both parents are in the home, parental absenteeism can still be a problem if both parents work. This is especially true of fast-track parents whose priority is attaining the good life: power, possessions, and position. In her book *Children of Fast-track Parents*, Andree Aelion Brooks identifies these parents as professionals who work to acquire. The fast-track term identifies their attitude about life as well as their lifestyle. Fast-track parents often appraise self-worth on the basis of their job performance. They come to worship their career and status as the expression of their worth.

Many of these parents sacrifice family time in order to get ahead in their career. Brooks states, "Both parents usually need to devote far more than the usual 40-hour week to the job. And timing is against them since the most intense years of child-raising tend to coincide with the years that are most critical to career advancement."[6]

And when fast-track parents *are* at home, life for the children is pressure-filled and achievement-oriented. Second-rate performances are intolerable to these parents on the job or at home.

Typically, fast-track parents both work because they choose to, not because they have to. The second working parent, usually the mother, is often motivated by personal career ambitions. In his book *Growing Up in America*, Tony Campolo explains that the high hopes many women have of making it in the working world seldom bring the desired results:

> To the contrary; most women found they had not so much escaped the drudgery of housewifery as they had entered the dog-eat-dog world of competitive capitalism, complete with labor disputes, office politics, and ulcers. Prejudices against women, furthermore, often prevented their upward mobility into jobs that offered more intellectual challenge, so that a career often meant little more that nodding yes to "Can you type?" More and more women who had forsaken home and

family for what they were told was "more fulfill-ing work" began wondering what they had gotten themselves into.[7]

The fast-track mother is also motivated by a desire to keep up with the affluence of the Joneses. But does the time spent working to buy things compensate for the time lost with your children that money can't buy? The mon-sters of ambition and greed often tempt us to sacrifice more important things as they drive us to the top.

Mothers Who Must Work

The fastest growing segment of the work force since 1972 is women with children under three years of age, having grown by 52 percent. By 1987 more than half of all mothers with babies one year old and younger were work-ing or looking for work. In 1988 65 percent of mothers with children under age 18 were in the labor force.[8] Millions of these women are forced to work just to meet the expenses of raising a family.

Many mothers are distressed by having to work. They know it isn't the ideal situation for their family, but it's necessary for their survival. In a national study, 50,000 working women were questioned, "If it were possible, would you quit your job to stay home with your children?" More than two-thirds answered yes.[9] It's usually this group of working mothers who place top priority on spending as much of their free time as possible with their children. I know several working mothers who have changed to home-based careers to keep their children with them instead of placing them in day care.

Day Care

Day care is a hot, controversial issue. Pro-family activists claim that tax credits for day care rewards parents who work and discriminates against parents who stay home to raise their children. Mothers who stay home and a growing number of child-development experts agree that children cared for by their parents are less aggressive, more patient, better behaved, more confident, more popular, more cooperative, and more socially interactive than children who spend extensive time in day care.[10] A *Washington Post* poll indicated that eight out of ten parents stated that it is best for children to be raised at home by their parents.[11]

I understand family financial problems and sympathize with parents who must work. But day care attendants just can't be as effective as a parent who molds her child's life at home—especially during young childhood, the period of his greatest vulnerability. Most parents agree. They don't want strangers raising their children.

For four years our next door neighbor ran a day care center in her home. Her garage was converted into a child care room filled with cribs, swings, and toys. It was a vibrant and colorful atmosphere. This woman's love for the seven little children who filed into her home every weekday morning was evident. But every time I went over to visit, help, or borrow something, I left with the same thought: These children are spending precious hours of the day during some of the most enjoyable years of their lives with someone who isn't their parent. The amount of attention they received there was far less than what they would get at home.

The Consequences of Growing Up Alone

The greatest price for our nation's shift away from the traditional family is being paid by our children. Divorced and dual-income parents are exposing their kids to the temptations of too much freedom and the pressures of too much responsibility. As child psychologist Lee Salk, Ph.D., says, "We hurry [children] toward independence before they're emotionally ready. We rush them and shortchange their childhood."[12]

Too Much Freedom Too Soon

When kids are at home while their parents are away they sense that they are free to do whatever they want. Even when parents leave them with suggested options and restrictions for behavior, children left alone tend to cross those boundaries because they love the temporary independence. Left to themselves, they tend to experiment with activities beyond their maturity level.

For example, look at the temptations that telephone technology has brought to the child who is home alone. The 1-900 phone numbers can bring recordings of rock groups, betting on sports trivia, and phone sex right into the home. It's not uncommon to hear of parents receiving telephone bills for $300 or more because a child has experimented without understanding the financial consequences.

There are other more serious consequences when children exceed their age-appropriate behavior. Child-development expert Erik Erikson explains that each stage of maturity and development carries with it certain privileges and responsibilities. When children go beyond their age-appropriate stage and take on these privileges and responsibilities they often become psychologically and emotionally disturbed.[13]

I counsel many adolescents whose problems are directly related to being allowed too much independence. The freedom they have while their parents are gone conditions them to feel that they are on their own. Independence is like a candy bar to a child. Once he's had a bite he wants the whole thing. Then when the parents return, the child is forced to suppress and/or deny his feelings of being on his own. Problems arise over the inconsistency of moving back and forth between independence to dependence.

Many of the older kids I talk with have told me that they wish their parents would have controlled more of their behavior when they were younger. Surveys reveal that only 2 percent of young people feel that they were over-disciplined, while the majority said they were disciplined about right or not enough.[14] Because so many young people are followers, I see the need for parents who are willing to stay home to give direction and exercise authority. Many kids join clubs or cults because of their desire to have rules and to be told what to do.

The Reynolds are a strong family in our church with three great children who have been very active in our youth ministry. They're fun, bright, social kids, and they love their parents. Recently I asked Mark, the youngest, about his parents, trying to learn some of their parenting secrets. Teasingly, I suggested that he rebel and do something wild like getting his nose pierced and his hair dyed purple. We laughed at how his parents might react. "My parents would kill me!" Mark exclaimed. Mark's response was humorous, but it was also an indication of his parent's supervision and concern for his behavior.

Too Much Responsibility

I recently returned from a trip to Haiti, one of the poorest countries in the western hemisphere, where our group visited villages and played with the children. I noticed in every village a strong family network. The extended family—aunts, uncles, grandparents, and grown siblings—lived within a stone's throw of each nuclear family. Many Haitian parents rely on their extended family to lend support to their task of child-rearing.

A look back at America's history shows that our extended families used to live in a similar fashion. But today it's different. Extended families often extend clear across the map, so far away as to be unavailable to help each other. This lack of family networking combined with absentee parents force many children to be responsible for caring for themselves. What's worse, many older children must serve as substitute parents, caring for their younger brothers and sisters in the parents' absence. Kids miss out on their own childhood because they're busy with too much responsibility.

A child living with a divorced parent often adopts adult responsibility by acting as a peer to his parents. He listens to his parents' problems and often gets placed in the middle between them. Ashley, an eighth-grader, told me that when she returns from visiting her father she is always questioned. "My mom wants to know everything: What's his new wife like? How much money did he spend on her? How often did he touch her in public? I hate it. But if I don't answer her I feel guilty because she pouts and mumbles stuff about me not loving her. I really love my mom; I just hate being a spy."

Another area where children take on too much responsibility is with the economic worries of a family. Some working mothers have to stretch their pay checks and rely on inconsistent alimony payments in order to operate above the poverty level. The poverty rate for children living in female-headed, single-parent families is more than twice as high as for children in general.[15] The economics of divorce often work in favor of the husband while the wife, who typically has custody of the children, struggles to survive. Kids internalize this pressure because the financial squeeze affects their lifestyle.

A Case for Stay-at-Home Parents

The pressure to succeed and to achieve monetary goals drives many couples to dual incomes. Raising children as a primary focus isn't as popular as it once was. The traditional family is losing ground. Hope for our children will only be found when parents reestablish the importance of nurture within the home environment.

I firmly believe that the best way to reestablish nurture is for one parent in each family, if at all possible, to stay home and raise them. I'm not interested in debating which parent should stay home with the children. Traditionalists campaign for the mother, while feminists argue that this cultural expectation keeps women from realizing their full potential. I'm not as interested in solving the role expectations of men and women as I am in protecting the dignity of the parent who desires to stay home.[16] The parent who makes this commitment should be hailed as a champion in a society that grants this role little value.

> *By devaluing the role of a parent who stays home we send a message that a career is of greater importance than the well-being and nurture of children.*

My wife, Cathy, longed for the day when it would be economically realistic for us to start a family. Her education in child development had inflamed her passion to be a wife, mom, and homemaker. Her desire and intention were clear: She would work as a mother if she had to, but she didn't want to. Her mother had modeled the role of the stay-at-home mom, and Cathy's positive childhood memories and experiences solidified her desire to raise her children the same way.

A couple months after our daughter was born, Cathy was asked several questions that caused her to temporarily doubt her motherly calling: "When are you going back to work?"; "You're only a mom? Is that all you do?"; "Don't you get bored taking care of a child? It can't be that difficult"; "Don't you want to do anything with your life?" The intention behind these questions was clear: Full time parenting is only for people who can't find anything better to do.

I'll never forget the night after youth group when an ambitious, good-looking 18-year-old girl began asking my wife a series of these what-do-you-want-to-do-with-your-life? questions. Before answering, Cathy asked the girl about her childhood dreams for her life. The girl responded that she had always been infatuated with the thought of being a model. In a proud but gentle manner Cathy said, "The same intensity and passion you have for being a model I have for being a mom. As a child I dreamed about becoming a mom, and now I have the privilege and opportunity to use the mothering gifts God has given me." Cathy's conversation with this girl made me realize that we must educate our young people to understand that it's acceptable to grow up and care for children as a primary duty.

By devaluing the role of a parent who stays home we send a message that a career is of greater importance than the well-being and nurture of children. This message is wrong, and the tragic proof can be found sitting alone after school in empty homes across America.

Our message must change. Young people as well as parents need to hear that there is great value in child-rearing; it's a worthy and gratifying role. When Cathy strolls down our deserted neighborhood streets, she recognizes that most of the mothers are working. And yet she feels great honor in knowing she is fulfilling a godly and noble calling by spending her day nurturing the child God has entrusted to us.

Kids Under Stress

Young people today are under more psychological stress than ever before....They are freer than ever before to engage in sexual activity, to abuse drugs, and to flout adult authority. At the same time, they are less prepared than ever before to manage these new freedoms.[1]

—David Elkind

Chapter 8

I met Sherry when she was a sophomore in high school. She came from a wealthy family and had parents who believed they were dedicated to her development. Her bubbly personality helped her win the office of class president. She was very active in sports, competing year-round and taking lessons. Sherry's real love was dance, and she made every effort to squeeze it into her schedule. The motivation behind her perfect grades was her parents' promise to buy her any car she wanted if she received all A's during six semesters of high school. Church was also important to Sherry, and she played an active role in our leadership group.

During her senior year in high school Sherry became addicted to *No Doz* trying to keep up the pace of her hectic lifestyle. During finals week of her last semester in high school, she unsuccessfully tried to take her life. Her brother woke up in the middle of the night to go to the bathroom and found Sherry's suicide note within 30 minutes of her taking over 100 pills. Her stomach was pumped, and her life was saved.

Sherry was stressed out, and she snapped. Her story isn't uncommon among teenagers. As I speak to groups of kids all across the country I ask them if they feel stressed out more often than not. They quickly raise their hands and sigh in unison. This overwhelming response should disturb us all. Kids under stress express it in many forms ranging from apathy to violence, including suicide. Stress may be one of the reasons that suicide is a leading cause of death among young people in America.

Many children grow up seeing adults—including their parents and their heroes in the media—handle stress incompetently, usually with violence. Kids often follow these models and react to stress in their lives with violence also. The result is usually injury to themselves or others and sometimes even death. I've watched teenagers punch holes in their bedroom walls in response to a stressful situation. I've seen kids under stress attack another person with uncontrollable rage. The United States has one of the highest rates of violent homicide in the world, ten times higher than England and 25 times higher than Spain. In a given year, violent assaults account for as many as 25,000 deaths, while the rate for nonfatal injuries as a result of violence is 100 times greater.[2] One has to wonder about the role stress plays in these statistics.

Volumes have been written on the subject of stress—it's a hot topic. I found twice as many medical articles relating to stress as to heart disease. Stress has given rise to a new field of science: stressology. We hear about stress seminars, anti-stress inventions, and graduate level courses dealing with stress management. It's a complex phenomenon, and it's affecting our kids and pushing them into adulthood before their time.

Stress: A Subjective Response

Hans Selye, the man who pioneered the study of human stress, defines stress as our reaction to stressors, the potentially stressful events in our lives.[3] Personal stress is a subjective response that is regulated by one's ability to adapt to various situations. For example, Scott Owens may explode with anger upon receiving a report card filled with C's, while Jeff Maguire throws a party for the same results. The report card is the stressor, and each student's subjective response to it dictates the severity of the personal stress he experiences. Since each individual is unique, reactions to stressful situations will be different. Some kids have stronger adjustment devices to common stressors that might lead to a breakdown in other kids.

On the outside, most young people seem happy-go-lucky, but inside each kid is a complex network of explosive emotions and fears armed for detonation. When these feelings and fears are tripped by the stressors in his life, he may blow up in ways that catch his parents by surprise. There are many outside sources of stress for each child. Their resistance to stressors is finite, meaning that constant stress will eventually cause a child to snap.

Kids Under Pressure

A word I continually hear from young people is *pressure*. Kids feel pressure from school, parents, church, society, and peers. Pressures not only vary in their nature, intensity, and length, but also in the way they are individually perceived. If a child perceives an event as pressure-filled, it *is* pressure-filled, whether it is so to anyone else or not. Parental understanding of childhood and adolescent pressures is a major step toward providing a nurturing environment. Children with a strong parental and social support system are least likely to experience the painful effects of stressors.

Many adults can't recall the significance of childhood pressure. They remember school as being filled with nothing but memorable moments, and they have difficulty understanding how school can be stressful for their kids. Aaron, a junior in high school, recently got into a shouting match with his father over the pressure of school. Aaron said, "I'm doing the best I can. You don't know how tough my classes are!" His dad replied, "School's a piece of cake. If you'd just try harder you'd do fine. If you want to know what pressure is you should take my job for a week. Now that's pressure!"

Comparing child and adolescent pressures to adult pressures isn't constructive; they are two totally different realms. A stressor that may be perceived as "nothing" by an adult may be mentally paralyzing to his child. For example, a father may laugh at his teenaged daughter for spending so much time primping in front of the mirror. But looking good for that special boy is almost a matter of life and death to her. As they say, puppy love is very real to puppies.

How Young People Get Stressed Out

Because stress is subjective, no single pressure can be

pinpointed as an exclusive cause of childhood and adolescent stress. Many stressors are unique to each individual, but I have observed eight daily pressures that appear to be common in the lives of most young people.

Pressure to Be Perfect

Kids constantly tell me that their parents want them to be perfect. They feel pressured to be someone they aren't capable of becoming or don't want to be. Unrealistic or misunderstood parental expectations arouse their stress thermometers.

As I was preparing to write this chapter I observed a beautiful example of this pressure in a McDonalds restaurant. A five-year old boy was kneeling on his chair and playing with the straw in his soft drink. He held his finger over the top of the straw and drank from the bottom. We've all done this; it's normal. But when his mother saw him doing it, she yelled out his name so loud that it caused my McNuggets to jump from my plate. Then she proceeded to slap the boy's hands while shouting at him, "You put your feet on the floor and sit up straight or we're leaving right now!" Every other child in the restaurant was running around like they were on a playground, but this kid had to sit up straight and not play with his straw. Now, that's pressure.

Another common parental pressure toward perfection centers around school and grades. Jason was excited to tell his dad that he was getting a B+ in algebra. Unfortunately, his father popped his balloon of enthusiasm when he said, "Why aren't you getting an A?" Again, more pressure.

Pressure to Succeed

The pressure to succeed elicits the attitude in our children that life is a perpetual performance. David Elkind says that young people are constantly performing for an "imaginary audience" that watches everything they do.[4] For example, when Janet tripped while walking up the bleachers she felt like crying from embarrassment, thinking that everybody saw her clumsiness. Timmy told me the other day that the entire student body at his school has seen the huge pimple behind his ear and is laughing about it.

Cultural and parental pressure to excel, achieve, and succeed backfires on our kids by burdening them with a fear of failure. No one enjoys failure. To fail is to feel stupid. People may laugh or turn away and not want to associate with us. The fear of failure is a common fear that is intensified during childhood and adolescence. While some kids use this fear to ignite their ambition, most are immobilized by it and don't try to succeed in anything.

We must help our children learn that failing goes hand-in-hand with growing.

Fear limits our desire to take risks. During the growing years children should feel free to risk and to learn from their attempts. But for many the fear of failure far outweighs any aspirations they may have to risk.

In reality, usually no one ever notices or cares about our kids' failures. We must help our children learn that their acceptance isn't dependent upon performance and that failing goes hand-in-hand with growing.

Pressure to Conform

One of the strongest pressures kids experience during the growing years centers around conformity. Kids find it uncomfortable to be different, so they work hard to fit in and be accepted by one of the many subcultures on campus. Being labeled weird or different ignites their fear of failure. This is why you will see similarities in dress, language, and music among kids. These trends are often dictated by an invisible majority that informs kids what's acceptable in given situations.

Though it may be difficult, we need to teach our young people the biblical truth that they don't need to conform to the standards of the world (Romans 12:2). Rather they must be encouraged to place high value on friends who accept them for who they are.

Pressure to Make Choices

Kids are really afraid of making wrong choices. Their experience in decision-making is undeveloped because they haven't formed systems of discernment which free them to make simple choices. It's been suggested that one of the reasons kids like fast food restaurants is because of the simple menu. Selections rarely change, so the pressure of choice is reduced.[5]

Since young people don't like to be wrong they look to others to make their decisions for them. Their rationale is to have someone to blame or to share the consequences with them if their choice results in a mistake.

This is especially true of moral decisions. For example, teenagers regularly ask me how sexually active I was before I got married. What they really want is for someone to make their moral decisions for them ("Since Doug, our youth pastor, had such-and-such an experience, it must be okay"). They get frustrated when I won't give them a quick answer to their disguised how-far-is-too-far? question. I don't want kids to use my experience to determine their moral marker. I want them to internalize and own their own biblically-based values so that, when they are confronted with a sexual temptation, they will have already established and personalized their own set of values.

This internalizing process occurs when we sit one-on-one with them and talk honestly and transparently about the pressures of being sexually involved. When they personalize their feelings and fears and listen to valued, godly opinions, they are able to form personal values they will want to protect.

Pressure from Home/Family

Every family is made up of differing personalities and styles. If family pressure was nothing more than the constant renegotiation of relationships it would still be tough. But the home is filled with many daily stressors for the child: parental expectations, siblings conflicts, marital conflicts, loss of privileges, divorce, family economic struggles, and troublesome chores, to name a few. As Chuck Swindoll says, "It's more dangerous to be a part of the family than it is to be in a war."[6]

Unfortunately, the one corner of the child's world where he should be able to rest from pressure can be one of the most stressful. When things are going well within the family the child has a healthy view of life. But when the family is struggling the child perceives that his whole life is falling apart. And the more dysfunctional or traumatic the home environment, the more stress the child feels.

Pressure from Transitions

In June, kids who are graduating from elementary school, junior high, high school, and college are on the top of the world. But in September these same kids are filled with fear as they prepare to enter the foreign turf of the next level where they are at the bottom. This transition and others that tamper with a child's security produce terrifying pressure (e.g., changing schools, moving to another state, selling a home, etc.). Studies have found that moves like these produce lower academic achievement and increase behavioral problems that show up mainly in interpersonal situations.[7] Both of these problems result in pressure from teachers, parents, and peers.

Pressure from Bodily Changes

A pressure experienced largely throughout adolescence occurs from the anticipation and reality of bodily

changes. Girls feel pressure from the changes in their figure. The onset of menstruation, breast size, and body
shape are constant sources of stressful comparison. Boys
feel pressure over height, penis size, body hair, and daily
spontaneous erections.

I try to ease some of the pressure about body changes
when talking with teenagers. I tell them that guys fear they
will never be able to grow a moustache while girls fear they
will grow one, and that girls are afraid they won't have
breasts while guys are afraid they'll get them.

Since consistent change is a normal characteristic of a
developing human body, it should be understood that children, and especially adolescents, are in a continual state of
stress.

Pressure from Emotions

I'm continually amused when I ask kids this very simple
question: "What have you been doing?" Their usual reply
is, "Nothing much."

I usually respond, "What do you mean 'nothing much'?
Have you been eating, sleeping, playing, studying, laughing, talking, breathing?"

They laugh and nod. "Sure, you know, nothing much."

There's a lot more than "nothing much" happening
during a given day in a young person's life. He plays a
variety of roles during his leisure, school, and family time.
He may start the day as an indecisive child who doesn't
know what to wear, and then take on numerous identities
through the day: a smart-mouth older brother at the break-
fast table, an outcast at school, a teacher's pet, an athlete,

and more. All his diverse roles require him to use different energies and emotions and cause continual mood swings.

Psychologists Csikszentmihalyi and Larson studied the emotions of young people by having them wear electronic pagers for an entire week. Every two hours the pagers were beeped, and the kids filed reports on their emotions. The results indicated that typical young people may shift from extreme happiness to deep sadness, or vice versa within a 45-minute period. In contrast, a similar study revealed that adult moods and emotions extend for several hours.[8]

Parents must keep in mind these rapid emotional swings and their controlling nature in their kids. Feelings change so quickly that decisions children make based on one feeling may not be appropriate an hour later. Maturity stabilizes these emotions, but until then, the pressure of living with inconsistent feelings will affect your child's behavior.

How Stress Affects the Body

When confronted by a stressor, the human body seems to trigger a built-in alarm causing the nervous system to respond. This response was first described and popularized by Walter Cannon who termed it the "fight or flight" response. Cannon claims that stressors cause the body to mobilize for action, preparing either for self-defense or escape.[9]

Once the stressor is identified, the nervous system takes over and performs thousands of complex procedures instantaneously and automatically to protect the body. Blood rushes into the chest and head, moving away from the hands, feet, and stomach. Muscles tense, breathing

---

increases, and swallowing intensifies. The heart pumps faster and the pulse quickens. Hands become sweaty and adrenaline races through the bloodstream. The body's internal equilibrium is as upset as the individual, and it remains in this state of emergency until the stressful situation is defused.

There's little question that stress affects the body. Many medical experts estimate that 50–80 percent of all diseases have their origin in stress.[10] Stressful events can play a significant role in both physical and psychiatric disorders. Prolonged stress or overexposure to stressful situations can weaken the entire body, making it more vulnerable to illness. Some of these disorders include acne, nausea, arthritis, cancer (is there anything that doesn't cause cancer?), heart disease (heart-related premature deaths are increasing), high blood pressure, gastrointestinal disorders, ulcers, headaches, muscle tension, jaw pain (TMJ), asthma, epilepsy, diarrhea, oily skin, gassiness, depression, schizophrenia, neurotic disorders, and childhood disorders.[11]

No good parent wants to see his or her child in pain. It kills me to watch my daughter suffer, especially when I can't do anything about it. When I review the list of illnesses possibly related to stress I feel burdened to provide greater protection from stress for my child. I also want to ease the pressure on her by withholding the stressors over which I have some control.

As a result of my study on stress I better understand Piaget's classic work on the critical time levels of children's development. When parents push their children beyond their age-appropriate ability they run the risk of causing long-term damage through emotional stress.[12]

Lightening the Stressors

It's obvious that we can't keep our children completely stress-free. But we can help them build resources within themselves that will help them resist the barrage of daily stressors. By helping our children in this way we may also save ourselves excessive medical costs associated with stress-related illnesses.

While it's impossible to define one way of dealing with the hundreds of stressful situations that arise during the growing years, I can give you some ideas that may work for your child.

Find the starting point. Stacy is a type A, high-achieving, often stressed-out junior high girl who feels driven to be the best in everything. I recently asked Stacy's mother what she does to help alleviate some of her daughter's stress. Her wisdom was enlightening. She helps Stacy discover the starting point of her stress. With immature discernment skills, Stacy can't always pinpoint what triggered her stress—and it's difficult to deal with a stressor when you don't know what it is.

Sit down with your child and list all the situations that cause him or her to feel stressed-out. Then try to distinguish commonalities within the stressful situations. If these can be identified you can begin discussing ways to deal with the problem-causing stressors.

Affirm feelings. As mentioned earlier, what a child perceives to be fact *is* fact to him, regardless of reality. For example, Shawn, a high school student in my group, believes that Christian guys must be perfectly pure in their thought life and physical relationship with girls. Shawn feels that if he has one lustful thought his Christian life is ruined. He believes this way because he's convinced this is what I teach.

I have spoken on purity and lust, but I've never required a lifestyle of moral perfection. It's a nice thought, but it's not likely to happen. I talk openly about how difficult the sexual struggle is and offer suggestions to help. But Shawn won't return to church because he's convinced that I'm asking for perfection, and he knows he can't produce it. I can talk and argue with him all I want, but I can't change his mind or his feelings; his perception has become fact.

Many parents try to deny their child's feelings. A daughter might say, "Mom, why do you want me to get straight A's?" The mother responds, "I don't want you to get straight A's, I just want you to do your best." But because she feels tremendous pressure from her mother to do well in school, this girl perceives that her mom wants perfection. Even though her perception is wrong, her mother must accept her child's perception and honor her feelings while working toward a better understanding of the problem.

One of the aspects I appreciate about recovery groups is their honest approach to feelings. Their rule is that feelings are neither right or wrong; they're just feelings, and they should be accepted. You may think your child is wrong when he says he doesn't feel loved, but your opinion won't change how he feels. You must honor your child's feelings even if it is difficult for you to hear about them.

Rest. Rest is a primary human need that must be filled. Even Jesus, the source of our rest, took time to be alone for rest and prayer (Mark 6:46). But it's difficult for a child to get rest when he's stressed. The rest he needs must go beyond sleep and include rest from pressure and responsibilities.

Kids can be taught about resting in the Lord. This happens when they see us doing the best we can and relying on God to do His part. We must model the confidence that God is God and that He knows our concerns and worries and will respond to them.

Reflect. Unfortunately, taking time for personal reflection isn't held in high esteem. Our constant busyness keeps us from reflecting, while the illusion of always having to be productive fuels a destructive stress cycle. Without reflection, projects can become more important than people. It's easier to be busy doing something than to reflect on our relationship with God or ponder the values we cherish.

When kids reflect they discover that even the small things in this world are beautiful and important.

Children can be taught to take time to reflect. I know what you're thinking: impossible. I realize that it's a difficult task. Young people have been conditioned to hate silence. Kicking back with the music blaring is their interpretation of reflection. But it *is* possible for children to learn to reflect. Kids from my youth group who have disciplined themselves to slow down and reflect have thanked me for giving them the idea.

When kids reflect they discover that even the small things in this world are beautiful and important. They don't take things for granted as much when they spend time looking and wondering instead of talking and doing. Reflection gives them time to evaluate their actions and ask personal questions about situations. Time spent talking with God increases as they understand their place in this world and the power of God's greatness. Kids can learn to "be quiet and know that I am God" (Psalm 46:10).

Develop an attitude of celebration. I'm convinced that kids who don't know how to have fun will live boring and stressed lives. If a child doesn't know how to play, explore, and invent, you can give him the greatest toy in the world and he still won't be happy. You can develop an attitude of celebration in your child by continually looking for and rewarding positive actions. It's difficult for a child to be stressed when he lives in such a positive, fun environment.

An attitude of celebration reflects an enthusiasm for living. The word *enthusiasm* comes from the Greek words *en theos*, meaning "in God." God is the source of energy, vitality, and power for those who have a relationship with Him. True enthusiasm for living isn't dependent on external pressures but on an internal attitude which is centered in God.

Space out commitments. Many kids are living their lives on overload, some from their own choosing and others from their parent's desire to keep them busy. I know a girl

who is on the swim team, drill team, and student government, has a part-time job, tutors neighborhood kids,
teaches Sunday school, goes to youth group, and cares for
her younger brother. Her parents wonder why she's lethar-
gic in relationships and surly in her response to authority.
She's over-committed, stressed-out, and tired. Parents
need to help kids prioritize their activities so they will have
enough energy just to be themselves. This will free them
up to explore and grow.

Confront conflicts. Many stressful situations in the lives
of young people come from peer conflicts. Kids need help
in confronting people problems that keep them anxious
and stressed. When proper conflict management skills
aren't taught to them or modeled for them, they internalize
their strong feelings from the conflict, often for long periods
of time, without facing them.

Kids need to learn that conflicts with people are part of
life. Even Jesus, the Prince of Peace, was involved in conflicts. He prompted conflict (Matthew 21:12-16), He resolved conflict (John 8:3-11), and He avoided conflict (Luke
4:28-30). Our kids must be taught proper ways to reconcile
relationships and deal with their peers instead of gathering
ammunition and going for the kill.[13]

Live in the present. I love watching the faces of young
people light up when I explain the biblical truth that they
are new creations in Christ (2 Corinthians 5:17). Kids need
to understand that they are part of an ongoing spiritual
process. Too many kids are plagued by their past and allow
those feelings to dictate their future. Christian kids have so

much to look forward to, but the burden of their past keeps their present life in stress. They feel guilty for what they have done and can't understand how God can still love them.

Kids must realize that the old has passed away and all things are new. This understanding encourages growth and promotes forgiveness. They need to hear more from us about the present and the difference they can make today as a result of who they are. I'll always appreciate the words of Martin Luther King, Jr.: "I may not be the man I want to be; I may not be the man I ought to be; I may not be the man I could be; I may not be the man I can be; but praise God, I'm not the man I once was."[14]

Serve others. When kids have the opportunity to serve it takes the emphasis off themselves and puts it on others. I observe this phenomenon every Easter break when we take over 100 kids to Mexico to minister to families living in homes most people wouldn't consider livable. I'm continually amazed as I watch these often egocentric, stressed-out teenagers leave their concerns at the border and help strangers with true passion. For many of them it's their first opportunity to care for someone in need. Serving gives them a global perspective of people who are in greater distress than themselves. Through serving they are able to identify a more realistic view of their personal abundance and become aware that some of their stressors are petty in comparison.

As much as we love our children we cannot protect them from all stressors. Life doesn't work that way. But we can provide for them an atmosphere which allows them to develop at their own pace. This often involves gradually loosening the parental reins that may be adding to their pressure.

The next five chapters will challenge you to take specific action to reduce some of their stress and provide them with some hope. These five key areas are crucial to meeting the needs of young people. My prayer is that these next chapters will help you take forward steps in your journey of becoming a better parent.

Looking Just Like You

The only way morals can be taught [to children] is through the moral life of the parents.[1]
—Bruno Bettelheim

Chapter 9

One of the many joys of being a youth pastor is the relationships that I maintain with graduates. I love to get together with them, catch up on their lives, and relive old youth group stories. After years of talking with grads who are now adults, I've become convinced of a powerful truth: Who I am and how I live my life has a greater impact on kids than any message I could ever preach. I'm not discounting the power of the spoken word. But when I ask grads what they remember about their years in the youth group, they talk about things we did together and character qualities they observed in me rather than the teachings I presented. Here are some examples of what they remember:

- "I recall a time we went out to dinner, and I spilled iced tea in your lap. I thought you were going to kill me, but you laughed."

- "I remember the day you came to my baseball game and cheered for me even when I struck out."

- "I'll never forget the kind way you treated your wife. I now expect to be treated that way."

- "I remember when you visited me before my operation."

- "I'll never forget that you allowed me to sleep at your house the night my parents announced their divorce."

- "You let me help you change a flat tire, and the car fell off the jack and almost crushed you. But you didn't cuss—I'll never forget that."

Think about the people who have had the greatest impact on your life. Did they impact you by their words or by their actions? Possibly both, but lifestyles aren't as easily forgotten. Take a minute to list the five sermon titles or themes that have had the greatest effect on your life. Now list the five most influential people in your life. Chances are it's much easier for you to list the people than to recall the sermons. People, more than words, impact people.

More than anything you say, the way you live your life will have an incredible influence and make an indelible mark on your child through his growing years. You are always communicating to your child by the way you live; your lifestyle speaks volumes. You can't expect the old saying, "Don't do as I do, do as I say," to work with your children. They will watch you and do what you do.

Children Follow Heroes but Need Models

Children love to choose heroes to look up to and idolize. It was no different when I was growing up. My heroes were athletes. I wanted to be like them, dress like them, and play like them (I was too young to want to make money like them). The infatuation with hero worship will probably never change in our culture. There will always be stars in the public eye who draw our attention and dollars. We are people with an insatiable desire to be like someone else.

One of the problems with young people and hero worship is the impersonal nature of the relationship. Chances are slim that children will ever get to meet their idols, and even if they do they will probably have nothing more to show for it than an autograph or photo. Movie, music, and sports heroes are too busy pursuing their careers to be accessible to the people who hold them up as objects of affection. And the fame of most heroes is transitory: They're on the top 40 one year and then drop out of sight the next. I want my child to have a hero who is more available and who can model reality.

You might want to be your child's hero, but it's probably more accurate to think of yourself as a model. You model life for your children on a daily basis whether or not you agree to the assignment. Think about your parents for a moment. What did they model when you were a child that you still follow in your life today? Be it good or bad, you are the product of their modeling.

> *Children who mature into stable young adults almost always have a caring adult figure who has been a positive model in his life.*

You are the model that your child can know and touch. This is an awesome responsibility. A young girl may innocently dress like her mom, but as she gets older the emphasis will move from the clothing to the personality. I see young people reflecting their parents' modeling all the time. For example, Daniel is a student in my youth group with a terrible temper. I've talked to his parents about it, and they claim they don't know where Daniel's temper comes from. But the other day I watched the dad explode at a referee during Daniel's soccer match, and the mystery of the origin of Daniel's temper was solved.

There's no question that children learn through parental example. Children who mature into stable young adults almost always have a caring adult figure who has been a positive model in his life. Here are some tips to help you with your modeling.

Measure Yourself First

As parents we must take a hard look at ourselves to see what lessons we are teaching with our lives. Below are some difficult questions for you to consider regarding crucial areas in which you are already modeling for your children. The list of questions is in no way exhaustive, but it may serve as an indicator for areas that need work in your own life.

1. *Acceptance of people:* Are you prejudiced? Do you criticize people you don't know who appear different from you? Do you show respect to strangers? Would your child say that you are accepting of people?

2. *Conflict management:* Do you deal with tension when it arises, or do you hold grudges? Do you share your feelings in a constructive manner during conflict, intending to reconcile? Do you take action to better a situation once conflict is resolved? Would your child say that you handle conflict well?

3. *Faith:* Do your children see your commitment to God? Are spiritual matters discussed in the home? Do you go to church as a family? Does doing God's will have priority in your home? Would your child say that you are a person with a strong faith?

4. *Integrity:* Do you exaggerate stories when talking to friends? Do you tell lies in order to get out of conversations or off the phone? Do you always tell the truth about your children's ages, even when it's going to cost you more money? Would your child say that you are honest?

5. *Love:* Can you openly express affection? Are conditions placed on your expressions of love? Do your children see that you adore your spouse? Would your child say you are a loving person?

6. Servanthood: Do you rush to be first when getting in line for something? Do you stay and help clean up after an event or party? Do you always have to sit in the front seat of the car? Are you comfortable sharing things that belong to you? Would your child describe you as a servant?

If you refuse to deal with your struggles and sin, chances are good that the negative consequences will affect your family for years to come. Look at the lives of Abraham, his son Isaac, his grandson Jacob, and Jacob's 12 sons. Sin that isn't dealt with may pass to the next generation.

Point Out Positives with Their Heroes

Most children have heroes they desire to emulate. You may hate everything your child's hero stands for, but if you constantly attack his hero he will get defensive. A good example is music and popular music stars. Kids love their music and music groups, and they become very defensive when parents criticize them. A child's posture of defensiveness tends to solidify his unity with whatever you are attacking. But if you make positive comments about his hero, your child may be open to seeing the negatives without being defensive.

I spend time with a teenager named Jeff who idolizes a rock star. I personally don't like the man's music, and I'm disgusted by the lyrics which glorify sex, pain, death, and rebellion. But I told Jeff I would listen to his music if he would listen to mine. So we exchanged tapes.

When we got together to discuss the music, the first thing Jeff asked was, "What did you think?" I made positive comments about the rock star and his band. I told him that I thought they were excellent musicians and had great voices. Jeff nodded in agreement, adding his own stories about the skill of the lead guitarist. I'm sure he thought he had converted me to his music.

By commenting on a few positive things about Jeff's music, I earned the right to have my opinions heard. When I later discussed the group's anti-Christian lyrics and immoral lifestyle, Jeff not only heard my opinion but agreed with it. Our discussions will continue because Jeff knows that I'm open and willing to listen instead of attack. (By the way, Jeff couldn't find one positive thing to say about the music I like. He said it makes him sick.)

Seek Positive Role Models

If you are a single parent, you may want to consider looking outside the home for additional adult role models for your children. There are also two-parent families where an adolescent may respond better to an adult who isn't his parent. I don't encourage parents to delegate their nurturing responsibilities to someone else. But I think it is good for parents to ask other adults or extended family members who share their faith and values to invest in the lives of their children.

During my years in youth ministry I've seen dozens of young people positively impacted by non-parental adult role models. I really like the idea of a godparent-type person who takes a concerned, active role in the life of a child. It's easier for children to accept someone like this when the kids are younger and grow up knowing him or her as a good friend. When your child is in the adolescent stage a new role model is more difficult to assign because the teenager tends to be more discriminating about who he will allow into his life.

I'm amazed at how many good people are willing to give their time in order to help make a difference in a child's life. Every church youth ministry should be staffed with volunteers who are interested in spending time with teenagers and developing relationships with them. It's usually within this relational context that a role model emerges in the life of a young person.

Take Them with You

This may seem like a simple suggestion, but more parents need to hear it. Since children learn through observation, parents can make numerous learning opportunities available by taking their children with them whenever possible. I received an invaluable education just by "tagging along" with my parents and my youth minister. I watched them deal with people, handle tense circumstances, and manage daily situations. The lessons I learned made such an impression on me that as an adult I have found myself asking, "How would Jim handle this situation?" or "What types of questions would my father ask?"

If parents waited until they were perfect before having children the birth rate would drop to zero in a hurry.

I have already put this parental modeling skill into practice with many of the young people in my youth group. For example, recently I set aside a Saturday to build a dog house for our dog. I called Carl and Todd, two high school students in my youth group, and asked if they wanted to help me, since I didn't know anything about wood, tools, building, or canine architecture. We spent 13 hours together that day laughing, yelling, eating, shopping, swimming (they both threw me in a pool and then jumped in), and building a dog house that looks more like Noah's ark.

The day was a success because I got to spend it with two guys who needed time with a caring adult outside their families. The reports I received from their parents confirmed the importance of our time together. I probably could have built the dog house by myself, but by involving Carl and Todd I was able to invest significant time getting to know them and letting them know me. That's modeling.

Be Transparent

I can't write about modeling without mentioning transparency. Children tend to see their parents and other adult role models as having it all together. Children need to know that adults have weaknesses, struggles, failures, and an emotional makeup similar to theirs. Don't try to conceal from them the occasions when you make a mistake, lose your temper, or say or do something for which you have to apologize or make amends. They don't need *perfect* models; they need *real* models. They need to see you dealing with life at your best and at your worst. (Just make sure that when they see you at your worst, they also see you responding to your failure with humility, integrity, and love.)

Transparency communicates hope to children. They see their parents as real people with real struggles, and this frees them to be real people. They don't feel the need to be perfect since their parents aren't perfect.

Before we started a family, Cathy and I laughed about the need to get our personal acts together before we brought children into the world. We laughed because we knew we'd never be perfect, and our kids were just going to have to live with our imperfection. If parents waited until they were perfect before having children the birth rate would drop to zero in a hurry. Failure and imperfection is a part of life, and you must let your kids see it in you.

"I'm Gonna Be Like You"

When you understand the powerful influence of your modeling in your child's life, it will make a difference in your parenting. Hopefully, as you apply yourself to be a positive model for your children, your story will have a much happier ending than the one told in the lyrics of the famous song, *Cat's in the Cradle*. Think about the importance of modeling as you read these words.

> My child arrived just the other day
> He came to the world in the usual way
> But there were planes to catch and bills to pay
> He learned to walk while I was away
> And he was talkin' 'fore I knew it
> And as he grew he'd say,

"I'm gonna be like you, Dad;
You know, I'm gonna be like you."

Chorus:

And the cat's in the cradle and the silver spoon
Little boy blue and the man in the moon
"When you comin' home, Dad?"
"I don't know when—but we'll get together then,
Son;
You know, we'll have a good time then."

My son turned ten just the other day
He said, "Thanks for the ball, Dad.
Come on let's play.
Can you teach me to throw?"
I said, "Not today, I got a lot to do."
He said, "That's okay."
And he walked away, but his smile never dimmed
And said, "I'm gonna be like him—yeah—
You know I'm gonna be like him."

(chorus)

Well he came from college just the other day
So much like a man I just had to say,
"Son, I'm proud of you.
Can you sit for a while?"
He shook his head and he said with a smile,
"What I'd really like, Dad, is to borrow
   the car keys
See you later—can I have them, please?"

(chorus)

I've long since retired and
  my son's moved away
I called him up just the other day
I said' "I'd like to see you if you don't mind."
He said, "I'd love to Dad if I can find the time,
You see, my new job's a hassle and the
  kids have the flu
But it's sure nice talkin' to you, Dad;
It's sure nice talkin' to you."

And as I hung up the phone it occurred to me,
He'd grown up just like me—my son was
  just like me.[2]

The Power
of
Encouragement

The deepest principle in human nature is the craving to be appreciated.[1]
—William James

Chapter 10

Y|ou don't have to be an expert in sociology, theology, or psychology to understand the simple truth that people need attention, acceptance, and appreciation. You, I, and our children fall directly into this category. Unfortunately, most people live life with these needs going largely unfulfilled. What we desire and need least from others is what constantly bombards us: negative input that tends to pollute our attitude and distort our hope.

Children have a strong need to be loved as they grow and experiment with life. Parents and educators are a child's primary sources of attention and acceptance, and these significant adults must understand that their encouraging words and actions can mold children into mature and responsible people.

Adolescents need to be encouraged for their efforts and understood during their passage from childhood to adulthood. They are longing to discover who they are and how they can make a difference in their world with their lives.

Much of their identity is established as a result of how they are treated and spoken to at home and at school.

If you want to make a significant, positive impact on your children in a culture that is rushing them to grow up too fast, you must become a fountain of encouragement for them. True encouragement is comprised of words and deeds that affirm the God-given worth and dignity of each child. The effects of your personalized encouragement on your children will be wide-spread and long-lasting.

Encouragement: The Difference between Mediocrity and Growth

John was viewed as an average kid in my youth group. He didn't have a positive outlook on anything, including himself. Today, ten years out of high school, his view of life is similar: "It's okay, nothing great, nothing bad, pretty average."

John came from a functional home. Like most kids, he survived school. Aside from receiving a dollar for each A on his fourth-grade report card, he remembers nothing extraordinary about his childhood. His parents weren't overly affectionate nor were they overly strict. They seemed like average parents to him.

John suffered through all the typical adolescent trials associated with living as a dependent with a strong desire for independence. His experiences included getting into trouble, experimenting with drinking, girl problems, and home tensions. He was insecure about his looks, constantly performing to gain acceptance.

John got married while in college and would describe his relationship with his wife as "okay." They get along but don't seem to share the level of intimacy they once had.

John's management-level job gives him a span of control over eight employees. His two biggest job-related complaints are low productivity from his employees and constant tension with his boss. He doesn't feel appreciated for his hard work, which has caused his job to become a routine and painful way to earn an income.

You might change a few of the details in John's story and find that it is painfully similar to your own life or one of your children.

To say that Torie's life is different than John's is an understatement. Torie was born to parents who continually expressed love and encouragement to her. Prior to her conception, her parents wrote letters documenting their positive feelings about her impending arrival. She has hundreds of photos and videos that remind her of significant family experiences.

Torie's teachers encouraged her efforts and affirmed her attempts at new subjects. They corrected her mistakes gently so she would continue to try. Her memories of school are positive. She remembers walking through the hallways where the principal greeted her by name, asked how she was doing, and listened with concern to her response.

When she returned home from school each day, Torie was greeted with an affectionate embrace. One of her parents was always at home to serve her a snack and talk with her about her day. She remembers her parents listening to her feelings before making value judgments on her thoughts and actions.

Torie has many great childhood memories. She remembers that laughter was natural and common in her home. Her parents expressed love to each other, which left her with a sense of confidence. Through positive modeling and teaching at home she learned how people are to be treated. Her early years at home molded her faith in God and solidified her values.

Vacations in Torie's family were filled with happiness. She recalls playing in the pool with her dad and taking walks with her mom while talking about topics like why bees have stingers instead of tails like dogs. She remembers asking silly questions (If God wants us to love, why do we kill moths with little white pills in the cabinet?) that her parents received with a smile and attempted to answer.

During college Torie met a man who treated her well and cared about her as a person. He respected her values, priorities, and opinions and communicated his love through affection, encouragement, and sensitivity. Their mutual love eventually led to marriage. Today Torie's marriage is still growing, and she delights in the fact that she and her husband care enough about their relationship to work on their communication.

Torie loves her job. Her boss continually reminds her that she is making a profound difference in the company. The people she oversees appreciate her leadership because she notices their good work and compliments them for it.

Does Torie's story seem unreal? Actually, it is unreal; I made it up. It's my sketch of the kind of life I would love my daughter to experience. Take a minute to paint an imaginary picture of what you would like for your child. It may serve to remind you of your role as a parent.

I see my role in bringing this portrait of Torie to life as doing my best—the possible. I do the possible believing that God—who cares more about Torie than I do—will do the impossible in her life.

The Weight of Our Words

From my experience with young people, I know that a powerful aspect of the nurturing for which we are responsible as parents is the spoken encouragement we provide our children. The following story illustrates how words play a role in accomplishing the impossible:

> The 1980 Miss America was Cheryl Prewitt. I heard her say that when she was only four or five years old, she hung around her father's small, country grocery store. Almost daily the milkman would come, and she would follow him to watch as he lined the display cases with shiny bottles of milk. He always greeted her with, "How's my little Miss America?" At first she giggled, but she soon became comfortable with it. Before long, it was a childhood fantasy, then a teenage dream, and finally, a solid goal. It all started with a word spoken daily to a young, impressionable mind. It became imbedded in the subconscious. It became a prayer and a reality. Who was responsible: the

milkman, the subconscious of a growing child, or God? I'd say all three, but lean toward God, because He created them all.[2]

Don't underestimate the power of your words. You hold within your words the ability to help your children feel important and have more meaningful life experiences.

Jesus tells us that our words and actions are a reflection of the condition of our heart (Matthew 12:33-36). It's disappointing to meet parents with hardened hearts whose children starve for true appreciation. My perception is that most parents are simply uninformed about how they can influence and impact their kids with the words they use. If you believe this is true of you, the following pages will provide some helpful ideas in your pursuit of doing the possible.

Running on Empty

It's no secret that kids run around today with empty lives desperately looking for someone or something to fill their inner needs. We watch them pursue all kinds of potentially harmful substances and experiences that they believe will fill their emptiness and cause them to really start living. But it's a frustrating pilgrimage since they tend to plug up their needs with things that pacify rather than satisfy.

Below I've identified three levels of needs that children must have filled by the encouragement of parents and significant others.

Level 1: Children Need Attention

From the moment of delivery children are given attention. Each child's world revolves around him, and he grows up believing that he deserves all the attention he gets. When he doesn't receive the amount he needs, he acts out in hope of fulfillment. This morning Torie wanted my attention while I was talking on the phone. When I didn't give her the attention she desired, she let me know about it vocally—and believe me, she wasn't passive! Tina, an eighth-grader who is sexually promiscuous, is still acting out in search of the intimacy she isn't receiving at home.

Dress, posture, language, mannerisms, and actions are the subtle (and sometimes not so subtle) means kids use to gain attention. Many young people will resort to almost anything to get their peers to notice their clothes, check out their style, and envy their possessions. Kids become pros at making others give them visual attention. They play mental games wondering who's looking at them and who isn't. David Elkind explains that a young person will form and magnify his own imaginary audience who continually watches and judges his looks and actions.[3] This make-believe crowd helps the child fill his need for attention.

Eventually kids regard the visual attention they receive as superficial. It fills the void temporarily, but the emptiness again rears its ugly head and a deeper level of need is exposed.

Level 2: Children Need Acceptance

Once the shallow thrill of being noticed wears off the

young person pursues acceptance. All the "toys" they used for attention are of no value in this new pursuit. The desperate hunger for acceptance compels them to join a few clubs, switch crowds, visit a church youth group, or learn a new skill hoping to secure acceptance with a desired group. With persistence the search eventually pays off. The kid will be invited to a party, accepted into a clique, or exchange phone numbers with potential friends. At the same time he hides his real identity because his new friends don't know him well enough to appreciate his authentic feelings. But the acceptance feels good. It fills the need and the search seems complete.

But after a few months of superficial parties and conversations, young people begin to tire of their so-called friends. Kids find it nice to be accepted by a group, but they find it increasingly difficult to be themselves around people who don't really know them. Time eventually communicates that they need more than acceptance. They discover an even deeper need.

Level 3: Children Need Appreciation

Children need to be appreciated for who they are as people. Many times this means risking openness. If young people are going to be truly appreciated by their peers, they must be willing to share their concerns, dreams, and passions as well as appreciate those qualities in others. I believe this is the type of relationship God intended for all His people. It seems that without appreciation young people are destined to be superficial and lonely in their relationships.

Appreciation happens when kids can share their true feelings without fear of rejection or judgment.

It is an incredible feeling to be appreciated. Knowing that someone loves you for who you are allows you freedom to grow. True appreciation isn't based on conditions or contracts but on a love expressed through a caring relationship. Young people crave this! When someone expresses to a child, "I love you," and appreciates him regardless of how he looks or what group he associates with, *wow!*—he feels affirmed as the person God intended him to be. He's finally free to shed his masks and be himself.

If you want to meet your child's deepest needs, you must be dedicated to encouraging him or her by expressing appreciation. Here are a few ways to do so.

Recognize the importance of your child's world. Every child has something in his world that is very important to him. This importance may not transfer onto your priority list, but when you recognize the things he values you affirm his feelings and show him respect.

Meghan came into my office sobbing. The boy she had been pursuing told her that there was little chance they would ever date or be a couple. She was devastated. And when she shared her experience with her mom, her mom said, "There are other fish in the sea, and you'll be sure to catch a better one." Mom's advice might have been correct, but her timing couldn't have been worse. Meghan didn't

---

care about the "other fish"; she was still hurting over being rejected by the one she wanted. Her mom's response indicated insensitivity.

You don't have to agree with the importance your child places on the things in his world, but you convey appreciation when you acknowledge their importance to him.

Honor your child's feelings. If your child tells you how he feels about a situation and his feelings don't agree with yours, don't put his feelings down. Remember: Feelings are neither right nor wrong; they're neutral and not subject to judgment. For example, you shouldn't discipline your child for being angry with a sibling; you acknowledge the feeling, talk about where it came from, and resolve the situation that's causing it. However, a child's behavior— what he does in response to his feelings—*is* subject to judgment. You should discipline your child for acting out his anger by hitting his brother or sister.

Parents wonder why their kids don't talk to them. Most of the time it's because the kids can't express their feelings without being judged and criticized for how they feel.

I believe that parents need to ask their children more how-do-you-feel? questions and allow them to answer. Once your child expresses his feelings, they need to be validated first (e.g., "Thanks for honestly sharing your feelings") and discussed later. When parents say, "You shouldn't feel that way," they are passing judgment which may cause the children not to want to express themselves.

Last week I met with Kyle, and he told me that he felt I aidn't like him for various reasons. I like Kyle a lot. But instead of attacking his feeling by saying, "Kyle, you're wrong; I do like you," I said, "Wow, Kyle, I bet that was tough to say (affirming his courage for expressing himself). I'm sorry you feel that way (acknowledging his feelings without passing judgment on them or him.) Maybe I'm doing something or not doing something that makes you feel this way. But I want to assure you that I do like you. As a matter of fact, I think very highly of you and love having you as a part of our group."

Appreciation happens when kids can share their true feelings without fear of rejection or judgment.

Catch your child doing things right, and be generous with praise. I was challenging a mother recently to begin encouraging her problem son, and her response shocked me. She said, "He isn't worthy of encouragement, and besides, even if he was, I don't know what I could encourage him for, since he screws everything up."

First of all, her son is worthy of encouragement simply for being who he is. Second, he might not be such a "screw up" if he received a little encouragement from her. I told this mother to start watching for things he does right and compliment him for those actions. I also told her that her tone of voice was very important to this task. Her praise shouldn't come across as sarcastic or condescending.

I want to give you this same challenge for appreciating your child. Catch him doing something right and praise him for it. If you give your son four chores to do and he only does two, what is your usual response? Most parents would get on the boy for the two that he didn't do. How difficult would it be to praise him for the two completed chores before reminding him about the others? If you like the way your daughter answers the phone for the family, let her know. If your son puts his dirty clothes in the hamper before being asked, let him know you are thankful. You may need to search carefully at times for things to praise (you can always thank him for flushing the toilet!), but the appreciation he receives from it will be well worth your effort.

Encourage your child in front of others. Spoken praise for your children shouldn't only happen behind closed doors. When you encourage your child in the presence of others he receives a double blessing. Children love to be appreciated and to have their friends and others know that someone believes in them and thinks they are special.

I'll never forget the times my mom and dad affirmed me in front of my friends. I can still remember my parents introducing me to strangers by using some type of encouraging tag with my name, such as, "I'd like you to meet our son, Doug, who makes us proud." Many parents introduce their children with a negative tag: "This is Cindy, and she's shy." And then they wonder why Cindy hides behind their leg. Or they say: "This is Bobby, our wild man," who lives out his title by trashing your home.

The words we speak to our children have a way of coming to life in them. Bill Glass, the author of the book, *Expect to Win,* says that 90 percent of the inmates he meets during his prison ministry tell him that their parents said, "Some day you are going to end up in jail."[4] It's ironic that they didn't let their parents down. Or is it?

Weigh your words. If you recognize the power of the spoken word, you will understand the importance of avoiding negative talk with your children. There is so much truth to the old cliche, "If you can't say anything nice, don't say anything at all." I don't know how many times I heard that growing up. I just wish I could have learned the meaning at an earlier age. The writer of the Proverbs said it this way: "Careless words stab like a sword, but wise words bring healing" (12:18).

Your child may forgive the careless words you say to him, but chances are he won't forget them. Negative words cut deep, and the scars remain. I still remember the teacher who commented on my acne in the seventh grade. I now know he meant no harm, and he wasn't telling me something I didn't already know. But his words pierced my heart and reinforced the negative feelings I already held about myself.

Write it out. If spoken appreciation won't quickly be forgotten, it's likely that written appreciation won't easily be misplaced. I'd be willing to bet that your child will keep any encouraging letters and notes you give him. A note of appreciation slipped into his lunch bag or left on the seat of his car will be a pleasant surprise during the day.

I have a file filled with encouraging letters that I've received over the years. When I open the top drawer of my filing cabinet, I'm either putting a new letter in or taking one out at a time when I need to read something positive about myself. There used to be a TV commercial encouraging us to send "pick-me-up" bouquets to friends and loved ones who need encouragement. Flowers are nice, but you can save yourself at least $20 by writing an encouraging letter to your child that never needs water, won't dry out, and will last for years.

Say it when you think about it. How many times have you thought something positive and appreciative about your child and then forgot to tell them about it? It happens to parents all the time. Instead of merely thinking about it, do something about it. A recent experience emphasized the value of this idea.

A few weeks ago I was driving around the city of Atlanta with my friend Lanny, trying to find our hotel. As we drove we began talking about our fathers. Lanny's father is in a nursing home, and he hasn't been able to speak for several years. As I listened to Lanny's story, I began to think about my dad, how thankful I am that we are friends and how special he is in my life. When Lanny stopped to get directions to the hotel, I decided to call my dad right then. When Dad answered the phone I told him that I was just thinking about him and that I wanted him to know how much I loved him and that I was thankful that he was my dad. For a few seconds there was silence. Then my dad said in a broken voice, "I love you too, Doug. Thanks for calling."

I didn't include this story to pat myself on the back and say how great I am, but to illustrate a point. If a 65-year-old grandfather can be moved to tears by simple words of encouragement, how much more will your verbal appreciation mean to a young person who is wondering every day about his purpose and significance? When you think of something positive about your children, communicate it to them right away while it's still fresh in your mind.

I couldn't write a chapter on encouragement without mentioning a woman named Marilyn Whiton who has the gift of encouragement. Her children are in my youth group, and she regularly expresses her appreciation by leaving a phone message on my recorder or dropping me a short note—and it always seems to be at the right time. When I came into the office today to finish this chapter, the following note was sitting on my desk:

> Dear Doug,
>
> I wanted to send you a note to thank you again for your leadership and love which you continue to provide for the youth at South Coast. . . . Our family appreciates you and Cathy so much.
>
> We love and support you.
>
> The Whitons.

This note probably took her three minutes to write and cost her the price of a stamp. But dividends from small investments like these can't be measured by time and money. Her unending encouragement and support is one of the perks that keeps me going.

I wish you could meet Marilyn's children; they are some of the sharpest young people I have ever met. I can share with you one of the secrets of the Whiton's parenting success. It's encouragement!

The Healing Touch of Laughter

The life that has grown up and developed without laughter, and without the sunny brightness which youth justly claims as its right, lacks buoyancy and elasticity, and becomes heavy and unsympathetic, if not harsh and morose.[1]
—Mrs. G.S. Reany

Chapter 11

I'm privileged to be an adjunct professor at a local Christian college. During finals week one year my class joined the rest of the student body in a chapel service. The speaker was an alumnus in her late 70s, a saintly woman with a beautiful spirit. Her only problem was that she had a great deal of trouble communicating. Each sentence was totally unrelated to the previous sentence. The college students were remarkably polite and patient with her, considering that they had no idea what she was talking about.

After ten or 15 minutes students began looking around at one another with nonverbal expressions that communicated, "What in the world is this woman saying?" A few giggles began to surface, and I was doing my very best not to laugh, because I knew that once I started it would be difficult to stop.

After a few more minutes the woman paused, giving the impression that her concluding comments would follow. But instead, with an intense look on her face, she forcefully said, "Who stole the cookie from the cookie jar?" As you might imagine, the students couldn't contain themselves any longer, and they broke out with laughter. I didn't want to laugh in front of the students and professors and appear rude. I tried with all my might to hold my laughter back, but I couldn't do it. I left the chapel service feeling tremendously guilty for laughing at a godly woman nervously trying to share from her heart. Even as I drove back to my office I couldn't stop giggling about how funny it was.

A few days later I read this proverb: "A happy heart is like good medicine. But a broken spirit drains your strength" (Proverbs 17:22). During my next class we discussed the humorous chapel incident. One of my students suggested that maybe God used that woman to inject the campus with some good medicine—at her expense—at a time when student spirits were drained. I don't know if that was the case, but I do know God invented laughter and joy, and on that day his people experienced both.

Good Medicine For the Family

One of the common denominators I've observed within healthy families is laughter. This doesn't mean that they have a comedian father who jumps out from behind the couch with a rubber nose and horn trying to force laughter. Instead these families have a home environment where laughter is natural and common. Is this description foreign to your personal family situation? Do you and your children laugh together? I'm not talking about sitting in front of the television chuckling through the newest sitcom. I'm talking about a laughter that comes from the heart and communicates internal joy and happiness.

If you want your children to experience the joy of laughter, they must see it in your lives.

As Proverbs 17:22 declares, it's healthy to laugh. I'd even go so far as to say that there may be something unhealthy about you and your family if laughter isn't present. Your children need to laugh. They need to feel that their home is warm and inviting—and laughter can help facilitate this atmosphere. Laughter in the home helps protect kids from the pressure of growing up too fast.

Take Your Medicine

Laughter promotes an attitude of joy, and people filled with joy are fun to be around. Your child needs to see joy in your life and experience it in his own life. An attitude of joy in the home can act as a defense against many of life's problems. Young people with smiles on their faces and laughter in their hearts interact with life in a happier and healthier manner.

If you need more healthy laughter in your home, you may want to implement some of these ideas.

Slow down. It's hard for a family to find joy and experience laughter when they are stressed out. A recent survey by the Hilton Hotel Corporation found that 90 percent of Americans spend almost half their weekend time doing chores or working at their jobs.[2] Does this statistic describe your lifestyle? If you are always working you will have difficulty finding much time to play and laugh with your family.

You may discover that the only way your family can experience the lighter side of life is to make a conscious effort to slow down your family life. Turn your weekends into short vacations. Even if you stay at home make sure to schedule some time to slow down and really enjoy your life and family.

I hope this little poem, written by an anonymous friar, will challenge you to evaluate the importance of the events you and your family are involved in.

> If I had my life to live over again, I'd try to
>   make more mistakes next time.
> I would relax, I would limber up, I would be
>   sillier than I have been this trip.
> I know of very few things I would take
>   seriously. I would take more trips. I would
>   be crazier.
> I would climb more mountains, swim more
>   rivers, and watch more sunsets.
> I would do more walking and looking.
> I would eat more ice cream and less beans.
> I would have more actual troubles, and fewer
>   imaginary ones.
> You see, I'm one of those people who lives life
>   prophylactically and sensibly hour after

hour, day after day. I've been one of those
people who never go anywhere without a
thermometer, a hot-water bottle, a gargle, a
raincoat, aspirin, and a parachute.
If I had to do it over again I would go places,
do things and travel lighter than I have.
If I had my life to live over I would start
barefooted earlier in the spring and stay that
way later in the fall.
I would play hooky more.
I wouldn't make such good grades, except by
accident.
I would ride on more merry-go-rounds.
I would pick more daisies.[3]

Schedule play time for the family. I recently saw a sign that
read, "Families that play together stay together." I realize
that there's more to keeping a family together than playing,
but play will increase the laughter and the bonding in a
family.

Many busy families must schedule time for play. I know
one family whose members are very busy, but they schedule two hours every Sunday afternoon to play together.
Each family member is responsible to plan an activity one
Sunday a month: play miniature golf, ride bikes, have an
egg toss contest, etc. It's not important to them *what* they
play, just that they *play*.

During times of play it is wise to teach your children that
winning is fun, but it's not as important as participating
and enjoying the company of other people. I come in contact with at least one teenager each week who would rather

die than lose. If he (90 percent of the time it's a boy) doesn't quit before losing, he'll probably complain about the teams being unfairly divided or that he was cheated in some way. Competition is fun, but when the thrill of competition gets in the way of others having an enjoyable experience, it has become too important.

Another idea for play is not to focus on rules. Allow your child's play to be spontaneous and inventive. Kids love to play and invent the rules as they go along, and they usually have a good time doing it until some adult claims that all games must have rules. Give the rules a rest and you'll find play being naturally fun.

Involve play at extended family events. You might begin a tradition that involves some type of play when your extended family gets together. Your children need to laugh with relatives of all ages outside your immediate family. The laughter shared at family events isn't soon forgotten.

At my father's retirement party I was in charge of the entertainment for the senior citizens. (As a youth pastor, I'm always asked at social settings to be in charge of the entertainment and to pray for the food!) I had them playing the same games I use with teenagers. As I watched them running (well, not exactly running, but moving at a pace a bit quicker than a walk) around the backyard trying to grab balloons and stuff them into a bag, I realized that play, fun, and laughter is something that crosses all age barriers. People love to have fun, and playing together at a family event will provide times of bonding as well as meaningful memories.

Play without your children. If you want your children to experience the joy of laughter, they must see it in your lives. You are their models. Set time aside where you and your spouse play together inside and outside the home. Sitting in front of the television and watching brainless shows night after night sets a bad example for your children that they may take into their own marriages. I'm not suggesting that you go to the park and throw Frisbees on a daily basis, but I do advise you to set time aside occasionally for a date night when you enjoy the company of one another and experience some type of play without your children. It will be great for your marriage as well as communicate a powerful message to your children.

Look for humor in the little things. People who have laughter in their hearts have a way of finding humor in the ordinary and common things of life. For example, my wife recently bought me a new pair of socks, and we laughed at the tiny plastic hanger they came on. We wondered if some people actually have tiny closets where they hang their socks.

I have a friend who makes jokes about the wording of some advertisements. He sees a sign that reads, "Drive-thru Window," and quips, "I tried, but I got arrested." Or for the sign that reads, "Ears pierced while you wait," my friend asks, "How else could they do it? You can't leave your ears at the store."

Thousands of humorous things happen around us each day, but most of the time we don't notice them. We usually view them as sources of stress or uncomfortable situations. But when we take time to think about these happenings, we often discover how humorous they are. You can help reduce your child's stress by sharing your laughter at the little things in life.

Develop family secrets. Most families experience humorous situations together that provide an amusing memory for everyone involved. These funny moments can become "inside jokes" for the family which will keep the family laughing for a long time.

My father worked for the Ford Motor Company, so we got a new company car every six months. Our entire family loved the smell of Dad's new cars. One night after one of my baseball games, I took off my dirty socks and stuffed them under the seat so they wouldn't stink up Dad's car, then forgot all about them. A few hot, summer days later when we got in the car to go to church, we were all grossed out by the smell. I had forgotten about the socks, and my parents had no clue. At first we thought something had died in the car. Dad sprayed the car with deodorizer, but he couldn't get the smell out. For about two months we drove around enduring the smell and fiercely complaining.

Finally Dad took the car into the shop. While detailing the interior, one of the mechanics found my socks. We kids thought the incident was funny and, luckily for me, so did my parents. My smelly socks soon became a family joke. Whenever one of us mentioned them our entire family would crack up. When we experienced a family problem, someone would say, "I wonder if this has anything to do with Doug's socks," and the laughter would quickly lift our spirits.

I suggest that you look for key words or comments from a funny family situation which you can quote at times to relive the humorous moment. No one needs to understand it but your family.

Be silly. Some of the funniest situations I have ever experienced have centered around being silly. Silliness happens when people feel free to drop their guard and allow the child in them to come out and play. There's no question that young people have the ability to be silly, but it's rare to see adults let loose and have a good time. Kids love seeing their parents act silly when it's appropriate.

Try injecting a little laughter into your family by doing something silly with them once in a while. For example:

- Leave funny notes for your children taped under the toilet seat lid.
- Put a can of anchovies in your son's school lunch.
- Rearrange your daughter's sock and underwear drawer.
- Have a contest after dinner to see who can eat their ice cream the fastest—with chopsticks!
- Make Jell-o in the bathtub.

As you help your children develop a good sense of humor, they may come up with some silliness aimed at you. You would be wise to help them discern safe pranks from harmful pranks so they won't glue your eyelids shut.

Do the unexpected. By doing things that are totally unexpected or unconventional you will not only surprise your family but increase their laughter. Some of my favorite family memories are of the times that my parents either crossed the boundaries of normal behavior or allowed us children to do so for the sake of sharing a good time.

I'll never forget helping my mom with the dishes one day as a junior higher and getting into a huge water fight in the middle of the kitchen. It went on for 30 minutes. And whenever another family member came to see what was happening, we threw water on them and welcomed them into the game.

Plan surprises. There is something about a pleasant surprise that seems to delight the heart. One year for my birthday my wife made a cake that was actually a water balloon covered with frosting. When I cut the cake it exploded all over the table and my lap. The look of astonishment on my face sent our friends into hysteria. It was a great surprise that I will remember for many birthdays to come. (I later retaliated on Cathy by jumping out of the closet and scaring her when she didn't think I was home!)

Planning occasional fun surprises for each child and for the whole family will help keep everybody laughing.

I want to challenge you to immediate action on this topic. Take ten minutes right now to plan some type of play or fun that will bring some laughter into your home today. Okay? Ready, go!

Maintaining Positive Memories

How seldom we adults enjoy satisfying scenes as we walk through the museum of our memories.[1]
—Chuck Swindoll

Chapter 12

I have always loved hearing my parents tell stories about their childhood years. I'll never forget the image I have of my father and his childhood friends clearing the weeds from a field in Kentucky on a hot Saturday afternoon in the 1930s so they could entertain a rival baseball team on Sunday morning. I can listen to my parents tell stories like this for hours, especially stories about their courtship (I still can't believe my parents once dated!).

I also love to be reminded of my childhood years. My mom tells the story of one vacation when I asked the whereabouts of "Mr. Sippi" while we drove through Mississippi. As the story goes, my parents laughed so hard at my question that our dog started barking. I gave him a breath mint to settle him down, but he choked on it and threw up all over my sister who was trying to sleep!

Everyone loves stories. We grew up on them. It's so important that we as parents cherish, document, and maintain stories about our children and our families. Yet some families neglect this vital activity, and the children pay the price. Many of the adolescents I counsel feel lost. They don't have a positive sense of who they are because they have little attachment with their past. Their personal sense of history is largely a blank, and their only connection to the past is their own limited memory. Most people find it difficult to remember anything prior to kindergarten. And yet, as a parent of a preschooler, I know that some of the happiest moments of life occur before a child is five years of age. We must help our kids remember these special years.

Making a Present of Your Child's Happy Past

I believe one of the best gifts we can give to our young people during their turbulent years of questioning their identity is a historical reminder of who they are and where they came from. This awareness can provide comfort in building a foundation for the future.

After speaking to a group of singles about relationships, I was approached by a 35-year-old woman who shared a sad story with me that I will never forget. Her most vivid childhood memory was of a hot summer night sitting at the dinner table waiting for her father to come home from work. Earlier in the evening she helped her mother set the table and scoop chocolate pudding into small bowls. While portioning the dessert she said to her mother, "I hope Daddy doesn't come home tonight so I can eat his pudding." Much later that evening she learned that her daddy wasn't ever coming home again. He had been killed in an accident on his way home from work.

This woman had lived for years with one dark memory of her father: a wish for his death that came true. She explained to me how difficult it is for her to get close to men because, from her bad experience, she feels that she has the "kiss of death." I couldn't help but wonder how her recovery might have been different if she had some mental photos of herself laughing and playing with her father to counteract her one overpowering bad memory. Unfortunately, she has no memories of him except for the one she can't get out of her mind.

Make sure your child's positive memories far outnumber the negative ones.

I didn't include this story to frighten anyone into action but to illustrate the power of the memory. By documenting positive memories of the past we can relive them during our present and future. These memories can connect us to our pleasant emotions from the past. Children have many pleasant experiences and personal victories that should be recalled during their stormy growing years. Our early years are also usually filled with monumental affection. Through recollection these positive feelings can benefit us today. They also provide us with stories that we can pass on to our children to show them what we value as important.

If your parents did a good job of documenting your growing years you should consider yourself fortunate. With today's technology and the availability of cameras, video recorders, computers, and tape players, there's little reason for a generation to pass without significant documentation.

Be a Memory Maker

Here are some ideas to help you maintain the history of your family and make an investment in the identity of your child.

Take videos. We try to video tape our family at least once a month, talking about significant events that have happened and documenting any new developments. We always talk about how much we love one another, and quite often do silly things to express our playfulness. At Christmas time we select the highlights of the year and edit them into one video to give to the grandparents and other relatives as gifts.

I have a friend who records himself talking to his three-year-old son. During the recording he addresses issues his son will experience when he's a teenager. My friend knows that his son may not listen to him when he's an adolescent but that he'll watch the tape. The boy will see the love his father had for him as a child and learn his father's values and ideas about living. This is a very creative way to educate.

If you can't afford a video camera you will find them fairly easy to rent or borrow. There are several inexpensive books that can help you learn the ins and outs of using a video camera and maintaining proper lighting. I suggest that you use quality video tapes and store them away from your television and stereo so they won't be demagnetized and lose their quality.

Write letters. After spending countless hours with young people who couldn't tell me if their parents loved them or not, I became convinced that Cathy and I must do something to make sure our children knew about our love. So prior to the conception of our first child I began to write letters to our future children. In these letters I told them about their parents, grandparents, the condition of our society, and my feelings about our future family. And as soon as we knew that our daughter was on the way, I began writing specifically to her.

Now every month I write a letter to Torie expressing my love for her, telling her stories about our family, and recording specific markers of growth she has experienced. I plan not only to read these stories to her as she grows up but to get them bound into book form for her high school graduation. I'm convinced that having several hundred letters documenting my love will have a major impact on her life.

I've included one of my letters so you can see the simplicity of the format.

July 7

My precious daughter,

Today I performed a wedding ceremony. After the service I went to the back of the church to look for you and mom. You were as spirited as always and came running into my arms when I crouched down for you. When we went into the bride's room, Lisa (the bride) said, "Torie, you look so cute. Pretty soon you'll be wearing a wedding dress and your daddy will be marrying you." We all laughed, and I joked that no one will ever be good enough for you.

As we drove to the reception I began to think about the person you are going to marry. I began to cry. Isn't that silly? I just love you so much that even now I'm concerned about who is going to take our job of nurturing you for the greater part of your adult life. I often ask God to begin to prepare the man that is going to be your husband. I'm praying that he is a man who will treat you like the queen you are. Your mom and I will keep praying, and we won't need to talk about this again for many years. I'm sure not ready to let you go.

The last few weeks you have been on a "Daddy isn't as cool as he used to be" kick. You are much more interested in going to mom than to me—except when I say the magic word: pool. For the last week we have gone to the pool on a daily basis. You are so funny. You cruise around in the kiddy pool. You're confident and proud of your ability to maneuver in the water. You let other little children know that it's your territory. You're not mean, just confident.

Often I wish I could have an intellectual conversation with you and talk about what a great mom you have. My love and respect for her grows on a daily basis as I watch her care for you. She is the best. She spends all day with you. She will let you sit in her lap and watch a stupid video (it's stupid to us, but you love it) over and over. She never tires of doing the little things. I guess you'll have to take my word for it that she's the best. I'm falling deeper in love with your mom every day.

That's all for now—I could go on forever. You are a joy.

Your blessed father

Yes, it takes time to write these letters. But ask yourself: Would I have appreciated a book of love letters like this from my parents when I was a teenager? Your response to this question will help you determine whether you will set time aside to write to your children.

Even if your child is already in his teens, it's not too late to begin writing to him. Hundreds of letters are nice, but a dozen letters are better than none.

Keep files of "little treasures." My parents did a great job of keeping the little treasures I created. They have a file drawer filled with my first drawings, report cards (I wish they hadn't kept these!), stories I wrote, and summaries of my athletic events. It has been rewarding for me to look back at my life through this file and relive pleasant memories. I have also referred to these little treasures when sharing with my present family something about my past. These mementos give them a greater appreciation for why I do the things I do and a better understanding of my likes and dislikes.

It's not difficult to keep your child's little treasures filed and out of reach until they are at an age to appreciate them. Make sure one of the files you keep is filled with photographs. Pictures serve as a visual chronicle of life's events.

Give letters with or instead of presents. When we have a birthday party for Torie, we ask the invited guests to write letters to her expressing what she means to them. When she is a teenager and is looking for love and acceptance from others, we know she will appreciate the dozens of encouraging and affirming letters she received from friends and relatives on her birthdays. Most everyone who shares in this experience enjoys this assignment because they understand and appreciate its importance.

If this is an idea you would like to use, I suggest that you request these letters without placing undo pressure on your relatives and friends to participate. We've found that some people have a difficult time expressing themselves in writing and would rather buy a present than write a letter.

It's impossible to protect your child from all negative experiences and bad memories. He will experience pain, and you must have faith that God will do the impossible in his life by counteracting the results of his pain while you work on the possible. One way to do the possible is to take time to preserve, in any way you can, positive experiences that will later ensure great memories. Your role as a parent is to be a memory maker, working hard to make sure your child's positive memories far outnumber the negative ones.

Love without Limits

Unconditional love... is willing to accept less than that which is perfect, even sometimes less than the best... and won't turn each and every issue into an issue involving personal acceptance or rejection.[1]
—Dennis Guernsey

Chapter 13

I learned in a graduate school counseling class never to consider anyone's situation as basic. The professor spoke about each person's problem and struggle being unique and specific. After meeting with Jennifer today, I really want to term her problem basic because it's one that I hear all the time from struggling teenagers. But out of respect for my former professor I'll call her struggle unique— but common to many.

Jennifer told me that she didn't feel connected with her parents and went so far as to say that her parents didn't love her. I know her parents well, and I'm positive of their love for her— the same way that I am convinced that Tom, Randy, Becky, and Melinda's parents love them, even though these kids have expressed a concern similar to Jennifer's. Just because they don't feel loved by their parents doesn't mean that they aren't. Yet their feelings are valid and real because they are based on their perceptions.

I believe that these young people, as well as thousands

of others like them, perceive their parents' love as conditional or dependent on their performance. They might say, "My parents love me when I do well in school" or "They are nice to me when I get my chores done" or "We don't argue when I see things their way." They grow to believe that good performance turns parental love on and bad performance shuts it off.

I felt this way when I was a teenager. My father's job required him to travel Monday through Friday during my high school years. His absence forced my mother to do all the teaching, caring, and disciplining for three children by herself. While my dad was out of town I was the only male in the home, and I felt the need to exercise authority to keep family life from falling apart. In addition to acting like I was the savior of the home, I drove my mother crazy by arguing with her every chance I got. As a result, our home was often filled with yelling, verbal attacks, and long periods of silence.

I remember times when I hated living at home. I thought the only time my mother loved me was when I did something that pleased her. My immaturity caused me to see any anger or displeasure on her part as a negation of her love. Though I gave the impression that I didn't need my mother's love and nurture, I desperately longed for them. I realize that there are times when parents don't *like* their children, but most parents always *love* them. I now understand that my mother's love for me was unconditional even in the midst of the pain of our arguments.

There are many negative results that accompany a child's feeling that his parents' love is conditional. The most common result I have observed is children who feel that they can't talk to their parents or be themselves because what they are isn't good enough to gain their parents' love. Feelings of conditional acceptance in the home is extremely unfortunate because children also feel this pressure everywhere they go. The last place in the world they should have to worry about being themselves and speaking their mind is within the home.

> *Does your child perceive your love even when his or her performance is less than you hope for?*

Another negative result of this perception is dishonesty. In his pursuit of love, a child may lie about his performance, since it's easier to fabricate an acceptable performance than to actually perform acceptably. Dishonesty can keep a parent-child relationship from growing and will create an unhealthy distancing in their communication, which is the start of a destructive family cycle.

I Love You—Period

The way to counteract the faulty perception of conditional love is to communicate love that isn't based on your child's performance. This is the same type of love that God has for us: unconditional. Unconditional love communicates, "I love you regardless of what you do." There are things we do that God doesn't like, but He loves us even when we do them. As we mature in our relationship with

God, we will do those things less and less. But during our maturing process His love never changes.

If you're like most parents, your love for your child *is* unconditional. If your son brings home a substandard report card you may be disappointed, but you still love him. Or if your daughter kicks the cat over the fence you may be angry, but she's your daughter, and you'll always love her.

Unconditional Love on Display

But does your child *perceive* your love even when his or her performance is less than you hope for? You must figure out specific ways to communicate your unconditional love to your children. I've come up with a few ideas to get you started. This list isn't exhaustive, but if you put these suggestions into practice they should help your children begin to perceive your love for them as unconditional.

Cut the comparisons. Many parents show conditional love when they compare one child to another, either a sibling or a playmate. For example, a parent may say, "Michelle, why don't you act more like your brother?" Comparisons like these bring about devastatingly negative results in parent-child relationships. They are simply judgments against a child's individuality. When we try to fit children into molds and boxes that weren't designed for them we must anticipate problems.

When I think about how we humans are constantly comparing ourselves with each other, I am thankful that God's love and acceptance for us isn't dependent on how we match up and compare with others. God sees us for who we are today and who we will be in the future, and He still loves us more than we can imagine. That's unconditional love.

When we truly understand God's unconditional love, we are free to be the persons God created us to be. The same process occurs with your children. When you affirm their God-given individuality and give them personalized attention without comparison, they will develop a confidence about living life and loving others.

Discipline without destruction. I recently watched a parent drag her child from a restaurant with rage in her eyes and condemnation in her voice. I felt sorry for the child because of the public embarrassment he endured, but I felt especially bad because his dignity as a person had been violated.

Unconditional love disciplines without destroying the child. The child's improper behavior will change within minutes to hours of him being disciplined, but a parent's destructive words and negative actions can produce injuries to his identity that may last months or years.

I know about the difficulty of controlling anger around kids—I'm a youth worker. But keeping angry responses in check with my own child is sometimes harder. When Torie was two years old she had this thing about hitting me in the face. It wasn't my idea of play, but she found great humor in it. After several hits in the face one day I was getting so angry that I wanted to smack her back. But I knew that my exertion of power and expression of intimidation wouldn't solve anything, so I had to give her to my wife and walk away from the situation. I've observed that it's usually in these types of settings that parents react in a destructive manner.

I heard one child-rearing expert say that physical punishment in any form degrades self-respect and teaches that might makes right, ultimately setting the punished against the punisher. When parents are about to lose their cool and explode in anger, they should calmly withdraw their physical and emotional presence to show disapproval.[2]

Realize that grudges don't persuade. Holding a grudge against a child is a manipulative method that is bound to create resentment. True persuasion has the best interest of the other person in mind. A truly persuasive attempt won't include forms of manipulation. When parents hold grudges they clearly communicate love which is rooted in conditions.

Another form of grudge parents often use is limited forgiveness. They forgive an offense, but then bring it up again in another conflict to use as ammunition. Unconditional love doesn't use the past to ignite pain in a present conflict.

Ask how-do-you-feel? questions. The best questions we can ask our children are ones that draw out their feelings. Only when we can get them to express their feelings will we really know what is happening in their lives. Too many times parents ask questions that elicit a one word response: yes, no, or because. For example, instead of asking a child how he really feels, a parent might ask, "Don't you feel stupid for what you did?" or "Aren't you ashamed of your-self?" These questions are worded in such a way that the parent will get a one word answer—usually the one the parent wants to hear. These questions aren't directed at the child's feelings but at how the parent thinks the child should feel.

Another example of a bad question is, "Why did you do that?" Most kids will answer in the only safe way they know how: "Because." These types of questions don't encourage a child to express his feelings.

If you want your children to express their feelings you must state your questions in ways that give them that opportunity. For example, you may ask, "How do you feel about the punishment you've received?" And you must allow your child to give his response before expressing your opinion. When you actually listen to his feelings and honor them as being real you express a powerful form of unconditional love.

Give "just because" treats. I enjoy doing things for my family and close friends that catch them by surprise. I'll buy presents, send letters, or do favors for no particular reason. When they ask why, I tell them, "Just because."

I'm sure you can think of several ways to treat your child to something special for no apparent reason. The real reason is that you love him or her unconditionally and want to do everything you can to communicate your love.

Children come to expect treats for birthdays, holidays, and special performances, and giving them treats on these occasions is fine. But I suggest that you give unexpected treats at times when your children have done nothing special, and let them know you did it just because you love them. This will help you communicate to them that your love and acceptance for them isn't based upon any condition.

Plan a spontaneous sacrifice. The words "plan" and "spontaneous" don't seem to fit together, do they? What I am suggesting is that you sacrifice something you really want to do in order to do something for your child. For example, you might forego a golf game and surprise your daughter by showing up at a recital you already told her you would miss. From your perspective the visit was planned, but from hers it was spontaneous and especially exciting.

I'll never forget the time my dad showed up at my ninth-grade football play-off game when I thought he was out of state. He called me the night before to wish me luck and tell me that he couldn't be there because of important meetings. I understood, but I was still disappointed because it was an important game to me. But he found a way to be there, and I was thrilled. My dad came to several of my games over the years, but this particular time his presence communicated to me that I was more important to him than a few meetings and a scheduled plane flight.

It takes a great parent to be willing to sacrifice, learn, and struggle in order to nurture his or her children.

There are times when you may miss events that are important to your child. As much as they can understand your absence, they still wish you could be there. Whenever possible, be there, even if requires a spontaneous sacrifice.

Don't stop loving. Easier said than done, right? You may be thinking, "Sure, Doug, but you don't know my situation or my child." No, I don't. But years of working with troubled families has shown me parents who are committed to hang tough with their children are the ones who later reap the rewards of their dedication. Your children may give you the impression that they don't need you and/or your love, but inside they are crying for both. I've yet to meet a young person who wasn't looking for love and willing to respond when he found it. When your best plans and programs fail, remember to keep on loving. Through persistent, unconditional love you unleash the power of the God of the universe to protect and raise up a child He cares for even more than you do.

When I play golf with my dad I sometimes hit a second shot if my first one was terrible. Usually the second shot is much better. When it is my dad will jokingly say, "Nice shot, Doug, but any fool can do it right the second time. We great golfers do it right the first time." We laugh (even though I know he's going to say it every time), my dad feels proud for hitting one great shot, and I feel guilty for taking an extra.

I've been thinking about my dad's philosophy lately, and I believe that it has a parallel in the area of parenting. Any parent can provide food, clothing, and shelter for a child, but it takes a great parent to be willing to sacrifice, learn, and struggle in order to nurture his or her children.

This nurture is provided with the hope that children will develop into strong men and women who will help make our world a place that values childhood and honors the God-designed pace of maturity.

I'm praying that you will work toward becoming a great parent.

Epilogue

T wo hours ago I finally finished writing this book. I'm really excited. Hopefully my life will quickly return to a state of crazed normalcy, for which my family will be thrilled. But I couldn't turn off my computer until I wrote about what I just experienced.

To unwind, I like to watch the children play at our neighborhood park. That's where I went while my printer spit out the last chapter of this book. I dusted off a bench and sat down to watch. It was more fun than having a center-court seat at Wimbledon or sitting in the dugout at Dodger Stadium. I was a tired, stressed-out adult being refreshed by the beauty of children at their best.

I had no idea that today's show would be so captivating. For an hour I watched, listened, thought, and laughed at dozens of children. They ran, cheered, fell down, swore, swung, spit, kicked, played, cried—all while racing around their fantasy land. But for several minutes my attention was focused on a little boy and girl who were acting out the roles of a mommy and her son. I wanted to inform the pretend family that I was an experienced daddy and if they needed me to play daddy I'd be willing. But instead I just listened.

"Tommy, come here, and bring me that stick. I don't want you to poke your eye out," the pretend mommy said.

"It's not a stick, Mommy. It's a screwdriver." Tommy knew that make-believe is an important characteristic of playing house.

"That's even worse, Tommy! You're going to poke your eye out for sure!"

"Don't be silly, Mommy. It's only a coat hanger."

I laughed as Tommy exercised his imagination trying to keep "Mommy" from confiscating his stick. She seemed concerned about his eyesight, but Tommy's stick kept changing properties until it became a harmless marsh-mallow. Tommy finally convinced her that he wasn't in any danger unless the stick *melted* into his eye.

The longer I watched Tommy and "Mommy" play, the more I could see God in them. There's so much we can learn about life from our children. I believe that God really wants us to enjoy life, and those kids were making their Creator happy. Their main intent was to play, and they were living life to the fullest.

You and I were children once. Now we are parents. But the good news is that there is still a child inside each of us waiting at the window of our heart, like a child on restriction, hoping to go outside and play. If you will allow that child to come out, I believe you will find the abundant, exciting life that God intended for you to enjoy. I also believe it will help you relate better to your children and allow them to experience the childhood God has designed for them. Fill their childhood with a knowledge of God's relentless love, demonstrated in depth by your own love. As you do, you will instill in them a sense of peace, purpose, and significance that nothing they may buy, smoke, or wear can match and that no addiction or injection can steal.

God created life to be a blast, even for parents. Don't just sit there; grab it with both hands, and run with it! And if you fall, don't be afraid. You won't poke your eye out.

Notes

Notes

Chapter 1—Whatever Happened to Childhood?

1. Tryon Edwards, D.D., comp., *The New Dictionary of Thoughts—A Cyclopedia of Quotations* (New York: Standard Book Company, 1955).
2. MassMutual American Family Values Study, Mellman and Lazarus, Inc., Washington, D.C., October 1989. Reported in *Family Policy* 3, no. 1 (1990).
3. David Elkind, *The Hurried Child* (Addison Wesley, 1988), p. 185.
4. Nancy Gibbs, "How America Has Run Out of Time," *Time*, April 24, 1989, pp. 58-67.
5. William R. Mattox, "The Family Time Famine," *Family Policy* 3, no. 1 (1990).
6. Anne Remley, "From Obedience to Independence," *Psychology Today*, October 1988, pp. 56-59.
7. Gary Bauer, president of the Family Research Council, from a lecture at Irvine, California, May 1990.
8. Stephen Glenn and Jane Norman, *Raising Self-reliant Children in a Self-indulgent World* (Prima Publishing, 1989), p. 8.
9. Barbara Bobejda, "Freshmen Reporting More Stress," *Washington Post*, Jan. 9, 1989.
10. Ellen Ruppel Shell, "Now, Which Kind of Preschool?", *Psychology Today*, December 1989, pp. 52-57.
11. Ezra Bowen, "Can Kids Flunk Kindergarten?" *Time*, April 25, 1988, p. 86.
12. Gaylen Moore, "Superbaby Myth," *Psychology Today*, June 1984, pp. 6-7.
13. Survey by Backer Spielvogel Bates, New York, reported in *American Demographics*, December 1989, p. 13.
14. From a Minnesota Department of Education survey of over 90,000 kids aged 11-18.
15. Sally Wendkos Olds and Diane E. Papalia, Ph.D., "Are Kids Growing Up Too Fast?" *Redbook*, March 1990, pp. 91-100.
16. Marie Winn, *Children without Childhood* (Penguin Books, 1983), p. 6.
17. Glenn and Norman, *Raising Self-reliant Children*, p. 13.

Chapter 2—Did We Know What We Were Getting Into?

1. Bob Keeshan, *Growing Up Happy: Captain Kangaroo Tells Yesterday's Children How to Nurture Their Own* (Doubleday, 1989), p. 173.
2. Chuck Swindoll, *You and Your Child* (Thomas Nelson, 1990), p. 55.
3. David Gelman, "A Much Riskier Passage," *Newsweek*, Special Issue, Summer/Fall, 1990, pp. 10-17.
4. Merton and Irene Strommen, *Five Cries of Parents* (Harper and Row, 1985), pp. 94-95.
5. John P. Robinson, "How Americans Use Time," *Family Policy* 3, no. 1 (1990).
6. Gary Bauer, president of the Family Research Council, from a lecture at Irvine, California, February 22, 1989.
7. Ibid.

8. David Elkind, *All Grown Up and No Place to Go* (Addison Wesley, 1984), pp. 93-113.

Chapter 3—Buying In and Looking Good
1. U.S. Census, 1950, 1960, 1970.
2. Chart by Cynthia Davis, "The Good old days."
3. Survey by Backer Spielvogel Bates, New York, reported in *American Demographics*, December 1989, p. 13.
4. Teenage Research Unlimited, Northbrook, IL, as reported in *The Wall Street Journal*, February 2, 1990, p. B1.
5. The Rand Youth Poll, New York, as reported in *The Wall Street Journal*, May 3, 1990, p. A1.
6. Teenage Research Unlimited.
7. Michele Manges, "The Dead End Kids," *The Wall Street Journal*, February 9, 1990, p. A1.
8. Art Levine, "Playing the Adolescent Odds," *U.S. News and World Report*, June 18, 1990, p. 51. Study conducted by Loma Linda University psychologist Durand Jacobs. (See also Adolescent Counselor, August/September 1989).
9. Lawrence Graham and Lawrence Hamdan, *Youthtrends* (St. Martin's Press, 1987), p. 11.
10. J.D. Killen et al., "Self-induced Vomiting and Laxative and Diuretic Use among Teenagers: Precursors of the Binge-purge Syndrome?" *Journal of the American Medical Association*, 255 (1986), pp. 1447-1449.
11. Suzanne Alexander, "Egged on by Moms, Many Teenagers Get Plastic Surgery," *The Wall Street Journal*, September 24, 1990, p. A1.

Chapter 4—Getting High and Going All the Way
1. *The Wall Street Journal*, May 23, 1990, p. B8.
2. Michael J. McCarthy, "Tobacco Critics See a Subtle Sell to Kids," *The Wall Street Journal*, May 3, 1990, p. B1.
3. Kathleen Deveny, "With Help of Teens, Snuff Sales Revive," *The Wall Street Journal*, May 3, 1990, p. B1.
4. "Monitoring the Future," a study by University of Michigan Institute for Social Research, as reported by Marj Charlier, "Youthful Sobriety Tests Liquor Firms," *The Wall Street Journal*, June 14, 1990, p. B1.
5. Marj Charlier, "Youthful Sobriety."
6. "Monitoring the Future," a study by University of Michigan Institute for Social Research, as reported in "The New Teens," *Newsweek*, Special Issue, Summer/Fall 1990, p. 59.
7. Mimi D. Johnson et al., "Anabolic Steroid Use by Male Adolescents," *Pediatrics*, 83, no. 6 (June 1989), p. 921.
8. *Chemical People Newsletter*, November/December 1988, as reported in *Youthworker Update*, January 1989, p. 1.
9. Interview with Stephen Glenn, "Creating or Preventing the Potential for Addiction," *The Door*, September/October 1990.

10. CBS News *48 Hours*, November 9, 1989.
11. According to a 1988 study performed by the U.S. Centers for Disease Control, as reported in *Reuter's*, February 1, 1990, and *Newsweek*, Special Issue, Summer/Fall 1990.
12. Barbara Kantrowitz, "The Dangers of Doing It," *Newsweek*, Special Issue, Summer/Fall 1990, p. 56.
13. Ibid, p. 57.
14. ABC News Special Report, "Making the Grade: A Report Card on America's Youth," September 14, 1989.
15. Ibid.
16. "The New Teens," pp. 50, 52, 54.
17. *48 Hours*.

Chapter 5—Molded by the Media

1. George Gallup, Jr. Testimony before the U.S. Senate Subcommittee on Family and Human Services, March 22, 1983.
2. Victor C. Strasburger, "Children, Adolescents, and Television: II. The Role of Pediatricians," *Pediatrics* 83, no. 3 (March 1989), pp. 446-448.
3. "The Family—Preserving America's Future" (a report to the President from the White House Working Group on the Family). Submitted to the President on Dec. 2, 1986 by Gary Bauer with the U.S. Department of Education, p. 29. (This was quoted from George Gallup, Jr., Testimony before the U.S. Senate Subcommittee on Family and Human Services, Mar. 22, 1983.)
4. Victor Strasburger, "Does Television Affect Learning and School Performance?" *Pediatrician* 13 (1986), pp. 141-147.
5. Glenn and Nelson, *Raising Self-reliant Children*, p. 42.
6. L.A. Times News Service, June 4, 1988.
7. Victor Strasburger, "When Parents Ask about . . . the Influence of TV on Their Kids," *Pediatrics* 2 (1985), pp. 18-27.
8. *Parade Magazine*, December 18, 1988.
9. Ibid.
10. Mary Talbot, "Are Teens TV Smart?" *Newsweek*, Special Issue, Summer/Fall 1990, p. 36.
11. Elkind, *All Grown Up*, p. 103.
12. "The Family—Preserving America's Future," p. 29.
13. Kenneth D. Gadow and Joyce Sprafkin, "Field Experiments of Television: Evidence for an Environmental Hazard?" *Pediatrics* 83, no. 3 (March 1989), pp. 399-404.
14. Ibid.
15. Glenn Ruffenach, "Homicides, Suicides Found to Account for 20 Percent of Fatal Injuries Among Youth," *The Wall Street Journal*, July 9, 1990, p. B4.
16. An examination of 20 field experiments on the short-term effects of viewing aggression-laden television shows on child social behavior was performed by Kenneth D. Gadow and Joyce Sprafkin, and reported in "Field Experiments of Television: Evidence for an Environmental Hazard?" *Pediatrics* 83,

no. 3 (March 1989), pp. 399-404. Authors from the Department of Psychiatry and Behavioral Science, State University of New York, Stony Brook.

17. Strasburger, "Children, Adolescents, and Television," pp. 446-48.
18. "The Family—Preserving America's Future."
19. Ibid.
20. U.S. Department of Education, cited in *Newsweek* Special Issue, Summer/Fall 1990, p. 36.
21. Neil Postman, *The Disappearance of Childhood* (Delacorte Press, 1982), p. 84.
22. "The Family—Preserving America's Future."
23. Postman, *Disappearance*, pp. 88, 97.
24. Dr. Ralph E. Minear and William Proctor, *Kids Who Have Too Much* (Thomas Nelson, 1989), pp. 32-34.
25. John Leo, "Rock 'n' Roll's Hatemongering," *U.S. News and World Report*, March 19, 1990, p. 17.
26. Ibid.
27. John Schwartz, "Stalking the Youth Market," *Newsweek*, Special Issue, Summer/Fall 1990, p. 36.
28. American Academy of Pediatrics, Committee on Communications, *Pediatrics* 83, no. 2 (February 1989), p. 314.

Chapter 6—Hurry Up and Learn
1. For a more in-depth understanding of the crisis of schools read Stephen Glenn's and Jane Nelsen's excellent book, *Raising Self-Reliant Children in a Self-Indulgent World* (Prima Publishing, 1989), pp. 26ff.
2. Stephen Glenn, "Raising Capable Children" lecture, National Youth Workers Convention, October 27, 1990.
3. Glenn and Nelsen, *Raising Self-Reliant Children*, pp. 29-30.
4. Survey by Gerber Products Company, Fremont, Michigan; reported in *American Demographics*, December 1989, p. 13.
5. Andrea Atkins, "Type-A Tots," *Better Homes and Gardens*, November 1989, p. 36.
6. "Cramming for First-Grade Finals," *Cincinnati Enquirer*, September 14, 1989 as reported in *Youthworker Update* (Youth Specialties), November 1989, Vol. 4, No. 3.
7. T. Berry Brazelton, *Working and Caring*; cited by Harold B. Smith, "Superkids and Superparents," *Christianity Today*, September 18, 1987, p. 14.
8. Smith, "Superkids and Superparents," p. 14.
9. Page Smith, *Killing the Spirit* (Viking, 1990), p. 25.
10. Glenn and Nelsen, *Raising Self-Reliant Children*, pp. 29-30.
11. Kenneth H. Bacon, "Many Educators View Involved Parents as Key to Children's Success in School," *Wall Street Journal*, July 31, 1990.
12. Elizabeth Hall, "What's a Parent to Do?" *Psychology Today*, May 1984, pp. 59-63.
13. Bruno Bettelheim, *A Good Enough Parent*, cited by Smith, "Superkids and Superparents," p. 15.

Chapter 7
1. Amitai Etzioni, Testimony before the U.S. Senate Subcommittee on Family and Human Services, March 22, 1983. Reported in *The Family:* A report to the President from the White House Working Group on the Family, 1986.
2. Viktor Gecas, "Born in the USA in the 1980s: Growing Up in Difficult Times," *Journal of Family Issues* 8, no. 4 (December 1987), pp. 434-436.
3. "Where Are the Parents?" *Newsweek*, Special Issue, Fall/Winter 1990.
4. Statistics presented in a paper by the National Commission on Children. For copies of this information write: National Commission on Children, 1111 18th Sthreet, N.W., Suite 810, Washington, D.C. 20036.
5. U.S. Census, 1990.
6. Andree Aelion Brooks, *Children of Fast-track Parents* (Penguin Books, 1989), p. 7.
7. Tony Campolo, *Growing Up in America* (Zondervan, 1989), p. 133.
8. National Commission on Children.
9. Beth Spring, "Having It All at Home," *Focus on the Family*, October 1989.
10. *Family Policy*, January/Februay 1989, Publication of the Family Research Council.
11. Richard Morin, "National Poll Finds Support for Day Care as Employee Benefit," *The Washington Post*, September 3, 1989.
12. Olds and Papalia, "Growing Up Too Fast?"
13. Campolo, *Growing Up in America*, pp. 119-120.
14. Joe White, *How to Be a Hero to Your Teenager* (Tyndale, 1984), p. 87.
15. For an in-depth discussion of the topic of working mothers, see chapter 4 in Tony Campolo's book, *20 Hot Potatoes Christians Are Afraid to Touch* (Word Publishers).
16. National Commission on Children.

Chapter 8
1. Elkind, *All Grown Up*, p. 179.
2. Howard Spivak, Deborah Prothrow-Smith, and Alice J. Hausman, "Children at Risk: Current Social and Medical Challenges," *The Pediatric Clinics of North America*, December 1988, p. 1339.
3. Hans Selye, *Selye's Guide to Stress Research* (Van Nostrand Reinhold Company, 1980), pp. x,xi.
4. Elkind, *All Grown Up*, p. 39.
5. Ibid.
6. Reported in *Youthworker Update* (Youth Specialties, 1989).
7. Bernard L. Bloom, Ph.D., "Stressful Life Event Theory and Research: Implications for Primary Prevention," U.S. Department of Health and Human Services, p. 66ff.
8. *Psychology Today*, May 1987, p. 56. For more detailed results see Csikszentmihalyi and Larson's book, *Being Adolescent: Conflict and Growth in the Teenage Years* (Basic Books).
9. Selye, *Handbook of Stress*, pp. 7-8.

10. Cecil Osborne, *Release from Fear and Anxiety* (Word Publishers, 1976), p. 15.
11. Most books on stress listed different varieties of stress-related diseases. For a thorough study of stress-related illnesses and conditions, see Clorinda Margolis and Linda Shrier, *Manual of Stress Management* (The Franklin Institute Press, 1982), pp. 49ff.
12. To develop a better understanding of Piaget, you may want to read Dorothy Singer and Tracy Revenson, *How a Child Thinks: A Piaget Primer* (Plume Books, 1978).
13. For a more detailed description of conflict management and how to teach it to young people, see my chapter on conflict management in *How Not to Be a Goon* (Regal Books, 1986).
14. Martin Luther King, Jr.

Chapter 9
1. Jon Stewart, "Bettelheim," *Parenting*, September 1988, p. 90.
2. "Cat's in the Cradle," written by Sandy Chapin and Harry Chapin, 1974, Story Songs Ltd. (ASCAP).

Chapter 10
1. Dale Carnegie, *How to Win Friends and Influence People* (Pocket Books, 1964), p. 99.
2. Fields, *How Not to Be a Goon*, pp. 80-81.
3. Elkind, *All Grown Up*, pp. 33-37.
4. Bill Glass, *Expect to Win* (Word Publishing).

Chapter 11
1. Edwards, comp., *The New Dictionary of Thoughts*.
2. Norman Lobsenz, "Do You Really Know How to Play?" *Parade Magazine*, June 3, 1990, p. 24.
3. Tim Hansel, *When I Relax I Feel Guilty* (David C. Cook Publishers, 1979), pp. 44-45.

Chapter 12
1. Swindoll, *You and Your Child*, p. 11.

Chapter 13
1. Dennis Guernsey, *The Family Covenant* (David C. Cook Publishers, 1984), pp. 6-7.
2. Stewart, "Bettelheim."

Acknowledgments

Although only one name appears on the cover of this book, many people played significant roles in its creation, and they all deserve thanks.

First, I'm indebted to my supportive and talented staff: Jennifer Hughes, who has been a great friend to me by loving my family; Scott Rachels, who has kept me laughing and warmed my heart by always asking if I needed help in any way; Jeff Reynolds, who has made my dream a reality by making the youth center happen; Jana Page, who helped with research and kept my life sane when it felt the opposite; Karen Page, who has given her heart to make me and my ministry more effective; and Keith Page, who daily defines for me the meaning of friend, brother, and minister, and who has made me a better person through our time together.

I'm grateful to Jim Burns, Dr. Edwin Ford, Rick Olsen, and Todd Temple for their assistance in the areas of research, critique, and direction. I am also thankful that God has gifted dozens of talented thinkers who have marked my understanding of children and adolescents, especially Gary Bauer, James Dobson, David Elkind, Stephen Glenn, Marie Winn, and Neil Postman.

In terms of personal support, I'm thankful to the following: the staff at Harvest House, who are committed to me as a person first and as an author second; my friends at Youth Specialties, who believe in me and my talents and have given me a platform to express them; my parents, Jim and Marge Fields, and my in-laws, Jack and Patricia Guiso, whose unconditional love for my family constantly keeps me going; the students and parents at South Coast Community Church, whose lives continually remind me of God's grace; and finally, my wife, Cathy, who is not only a great editor, supporter, and encourager but a model wife and the best mom alive—I love you.

Help for Effective
Parenting in the 90s

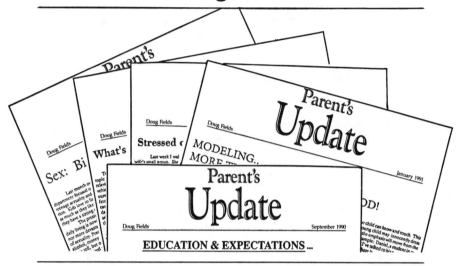

Parent's Update provides the timely information today's parents need to raise healthy children in our rapidly changing world:

- Valuable research on contemporary trends
- How-to ideas for creating a healthy home atmosphere
- Penetrating insight to understanding your child's world
- Current resources—where to go when you need help.

For *Parent's Update* subscription information, please send a self-addressed, stamped envelope, your name and address (including zip code) to:

> *Parent's Update*
> P.O. Box 316
> Corona Del Mar, CA 92625